Fun with Paper Crafts

Marilynne Oskamp

CANTECLEER

Preface

For the last several years I have had the opportunity to play with the 7 paper crafts featured in this book. I tried each of the crafts separately however; as I became familiar with a new craft I was quick to combine it with the other crafts I already knew. The results I believe speak for themselves!

I would like to acknowledge all of the different craft designers for their amazing talents. They are constantly conceiving new ideas and designing new products for their individual crafts. Many of the products and techniques are so versatile that they are used frequently throughout the book and you will be amazed at what you can do with them.

A special thank-you to my mother for her assistance in designing two beautiful chapters featuring parchment paper craft combined with other techniques.

In this book I have tried to incorporate designs for all seasons, designs for special occasions and designs suitable for all family members from young to old. All of the materials used to make the projects are available through Ecstasy Crafts Inc. if you are unable to find supplies at your local retailer. The item/order number is listed beside each product for easy ordering by your local store or on-line.

Finally, I hope this idea and pattern book brings you many hours of crafting pleasure and inspires you to combine all of your favorite paper crafts!

Marilynne

General Hints Before you Begin

Each craft technique has a set of General Instructions and materials required. Please refer to these instructions before beginning a project and as often as necessary to complete the project. The General instructions contain more details about the specific techniques and key points to remember. Each chapter indicates the sets of the General instructions that you may wish to refer to for the project series. An asterisk * in the specific project instructions will prompt you to refer to these General Instructions for more detailed explanations.

The General Instructions for each of the techniques also contain a list of the basic materials required for each craft. The individual chapters list the specific materials required for each series at the beginning of the chapter. These specific chapter lists of materials required do not include the basic supplies required for each craft to reduce repetition.

Before you begin remember to:
• Sit comfortably making sure that your chair is the right height for your table
• Have good lighting in your work area
• Work on a flat, smooth surface

Every attempt was made to ensure the instructions are as detailed as possible, however, if you cannot understand a technique or how to complete a project please email me at info@ecstasycrafts.com and I will be happy to assist you!

I hope you enjoy making the projects in this book and I wish you much success!

Marilynne

General Instructions for Embroidery on Paper

Erica Fortgens of the Netherlands developed the craft of Embroidery on Paper. It is a craft that uses the basic techniques of embroidery however; they have been modified for use with paper products. Patterns are pierced into the paper and then are used to embroider with regular embroidery floss, rayon machine embroidery thread or metallic thread. The craft is simple and suitable for all ages. Embroidery on paper may be used to create cards, gift tags, picture frames, memory pages or whatever you can imagine! Regardless of how you wish to incorporate the technique of embroidery on paper into your crafting projects you will be amazed at the beautiful results!

Key Points

When using patterns from a book, you should first photocopy the pattern and then use the photocopied pattern to pierce through onto your card stock.

Always pierce your pattern on top of a piercing pad to allow the tool to penetrate while protecting your work surface.

Small dots on a pattern are pierced using the very fine Erica's Piercing Tool and the larger dots are pierced using the Erica's coarse piercing tool.

The larger dots are located usually in the centers of flowers or bottom of leaves etc. where many threads need to pass through thus requiring a larger hole.

Use embroidery floss, rayon machine embroidery thread (40 weight) or metallic thread.

Basic Materials Required

- Erica's very fine piercing tool (EF0007)
- Erica's coarse piercing tool (EF0009)
- Piercing Pad (1419)
- Needle (the thinnest needle possible with a small eye in the needle)
- Thread (embroidery floss, rayon machine embroidery thread or metallic thread)
- Needle Threader (especially for metallic thread)
- Scissors
- Cello-tape
- Double-sided tape or glue stick

Generally you will require a double strand of thread when using embroidery floss or rayon thread. A double strand is a single thread folded in half.

It is important that you work in the order of the holes i.e. always go to the next hole in one direction, as this allows the threads to lie next to each other. It is also important that the center hole in flowers or other designs be large enough to allow all of the threads to lie flat and not bunch up. Often you will be left with a tiny hole in the center of the threads.

Occasionally you will need to increase the size of your hole after you have started embroidering....this is done by gently inserting the coarse piercing tool into the center of the flower (in the center of the threads) and increase the size of the hole. You may need to gently rotate the coarse needle tool to incre-ase the size of the hole.

When using the multipurpose stencils… remember to **save** the packaging, as there are instructions and diagrams on the back, there also is a picture of the whole stencil to give you ideas!

The stencils have patterns on them as well. Usually a line in a pattern repre-sents the thread in the final design. Some numbers on the stencils indicate how to embroider string art designs by following the numbers i.e. 1 to 2 to 3 to 4 etc.

Instructions

Place your pattern on top of card stock in the correct position and tape to the card stock using cello-tape. Place the card stock on top of a piercing pad.

Using the Erica fine and coarse piercing tools pierce through the photocopied pattern into your card stock.

Completely pierce your pattern. When you are finished hold it up to the light to see if you missed any holes before removing the pattern.

Satin Stitch: Take your needle (should be small and thin to ensure that the holes you pierced do not increase in size as you embroider) and thread, then coming from the back of the cardstock, pull the needle and thread up through a hole labeled as #1 or in the center of a flower or bottom of a leaf etc.

Draw the thread through until there is a small amount left at the back and then using cello-tape, tape the ends to the card stock. Do not knot. Eventually all of the threads will be covered with another piece of card stock.

Draw the thread through any one of the holes surrounding the flower or pat-tern coming back up through the first hole. Go to the next hole beside the first hole around the flower or leaf design. Continue until all holes have been used for embroidery.

Stem Stitch: The stem stitch is another stitch that is often used in embroidery on paper designs. For this stitch see the dia-gram. Insert the needle from the back at hole 1 and pull the thread to hole 2 where

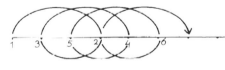

the needle is put down through the hole. Go along the back to hole 3 and pull thread to hole 4. Go along the back to hole 5 and pull the thread to hole 6. Continue in this manner as indicated on the diagram skipping two holes on the front each time and one hole on the back. For small curves skip only one hole. Remember to always come up on the same side (usually the inside of the curve however, some patterns are scalloped so sometimes you will be on the inside edge other times the outside edge….just be consistent). You may wish to pull the previous thread away with your thumb in order not to grab threads from the previous stitch.

Finishing the card: Cut another piece of card stock the size of the card and attach using double-sided tape or a glue stick to the back of the card to cover the threads. Sometimes you may do embroidery on an item that is then taped or glued to another piece of card stock hiding the threads.

General Instructions for Iris Folding

Iris Folding is a craft technique that was developed in Holland by Maruscha Gaasenbeek and Tine Beauveser. It combines folded paper strips of different colors into a spiral pattern to create unique designs. There are several pattern books available to make fruit, leaves, sailboats, Christmas designs etc. Iris folding is simple yet creates very intricate looking designs for cards and scrapbooks.

Key Points

Iris Folding should be done using thin papers to ensure that the design does not become too bulky.

Regular memory book paper is too thick. Papers to use should almost be as thin as wrapping paper.

The Iris Folding Paper Packs available are great, as they have already combined six different coordinating designs of thin paper as well as two foil pages together!

Instructions for patterns found in this book

Trace the outline of the pattern onto card stock using a light box.

Cut out the outline of your design in your card stock with a hobby knife.

Basic Materials required

- Scissors and ruler to cut paper strips or
- Paper cutter (optional)
- Iris Folding Papers or similar papers
- Light box (or if you have a glass table put a light underneath and you should be able to trace your design)
- Holographic paper or ribbon
- Hobby knife
- Cutting mat
- Cello-tape

Choose the number of different coordinating papers as described in the instructions for the card.

Cut paper strips to size again according to individual card instructions.

Fold your paper strips in half (length-wise) with the colored side facing outwards.

Place your cut out card on top of your pattern front side down.

Decide the order in which you wish to place your paper strips (i.e. what color will lie against another color).

Starting at #1, take the colored paper strip you wish to begin with and place the folded edge along line #1. Cut to size…leaving a small amount at each edge to overlap the card stock and tape in place using cello tape.

Take the second colored paper strip you wish to use and place the folded edge along line #2, cut to size and tape in place.

Continue in this manner until you have used one of each of the colored paper strips.

The next colored paper strip will be the same as you used for #1, the following one will be the same as #2 etc.

Continue rotating the colored paper strips in the same manner until you have filled in all of the numbers.

Over the center hole place a fancy piece of foil or holographic paper to accent your design.

Turn your card over and admire your design!

Finish the card by attaching your folded design to a card or attaching a cover sheet over the back of the folded design.

General Instructions for Ornare Paper Piercing

Ornare uses paper piercing to create designs on paper. You may use printed designs in pattern books* or metal templates of specific designs which may be used over and over again. Ornare templates have been used throughout this book to create or enhance the projects. The template used for each design will be noted in the materials used. Many papers may be used for paper piercing from card stock to lightweight papers to vellum.

Key Points

Always work from the **back** of your project to have the raised design on the front. Thus, remember when you want the final result to have the upper left corner enhanced with an Ornare design then because you are piercing from the back you will need to place the template in the upper right hand corner when piercing.

Basic Materials Required
- Ornare piercing tool (PR0100)
- Piercing pad (1419)
- Ornare template or pattern

Always use the specific Ornare piercing tool. The Ornare piercing tool is of a medium width and creates holes of the appropriate size.

Attempt to hold the Ornare piercing tool at a 90° angle or upright while piercing as this will ensure evenly spaced holes.

Do not just pierce with the tip of the piercing tool. The tip of the piercing tool is smaller than the remainder of the shaft thus holes will be uneven. Ensure you pierce deep enough to make holes the width of the shaft of the tool.

Always pierce your pattern on top of a piercing pad to allow the tool to penetrate while protecting your work surface.

Instructions

Place the Ornare template that you are using on the back of your paper. Tape in place using cello-tape. Ensure that you have the correct placement for the final design (see Key Point second bullet).

Using the Ornare piercing tool, pierce all of the holes of the design you wish to use.

Hold the piercing tool upright and pierce deep enough to ensure the holes are the same size (Key Point fifth bullet).

Completely pierce the design. Before removing the template from your paper, hold it up to the light to ensure that you have not missed any holes. If you have missed any holes pierce them and then remove the template.

General Instructions for Papuela Paper Weaving

Nellie Snellen of the Netherlands developed "Papuela" the craft of paper weaving. In this craft paper strips are woven into precut designs to create unique woven patterns on cards or scrapbook pages. There are many template designs available including caning or lattice weaving patterns that have been used frequently in this book.

Key Points

When cutting the weaving pattern into your card stock ensure that you have a sharp hobby knife

Insert the knife at a 45-degree angle into the template slit to be cut, ensure that you cut from the tip to the end.

It works best if you bring the blade up to a 90-degree angle and then even move it further so that the tip of the blade is almost facing upwards. This technique will ensure that you have cut the entire length of the slit making the weaving process easier.

When you thread the flat metal Papuela needle, first cut a small piece of the paper strip off i.e. cut in half for approximately 1.5 cm or $^1/_2$ ". Use this thin end of the Papuela paper strip to thread the needle.

Basic Materials Required

- Papuela template (see specific project instructions)
- Papuela Weaving strips a variety of color palettes available (see specific project instructions)
- Papuela weaving needles: small (5) (PU1001), or large needle (PU1004)
- Hobby knife (sharp)
- Cutting mat (IC1002)
- Scissors
- Cello-tape

To thread the needle, hold the eye of the needle closest to you. Place the thin end of the strip in the farthest hole from you then fold it over the small separation of the holes and down through the hole closest to you. Ensure that the paper strip lies flat to minimize the thickness of the threaded needle to make the weaving process easier.

Always weave one slit at a time except when doing the lattice weaving.

Use the long Papuela needle for the lattice weaving. The longer needle allows you to easily weave over and under the existing paper strips and enter the appropriate slit on the opposite side.

Work from the center of the design out towards the edges... this seems to allow easier spacing.

Save the packaging of your template as on the back it shows you the different designs that are available on different templates and it also gives you some basic instructions.

Instructions

Place your Papuela template on top of your cardstock and tape in place using cello-tape.

Cut the weaving design (slits) into your cardstock using a very sharp hobby knife on a cutting mat.

Ensure that you cut the entire weaving design before removing the template. (Once again hold it up to the light to see if you missed anything.)

Thread your needle with a Papuela paper strip (see above).

From the back of the card stock, slip the needle through the first slit of the design. Gently pull the paper strip through leaving enough at the back so it does not slip out. It seems to work best if you angle the needle away from you. Slip the needle into the next slit and pull the needle and paper strip to the back of the cardstock again. It seems to work best in this direction if you angle the needle towards you when pulling it through.

Bring the needle back up through the next slit according to the pattern and continue in the same fashion until you have completed the row. Place the design front side down on the table and gently pull the paper strip through the holes so that only a small amount is left to tape down at the beginning of the row. Now cut off the paper strip so that there is a small amount available to eventually tape down.

Move to the next row either to the right or left of the center. Complete in the same fashion. When you have completely finished the design, tape the small ends of the paper strips to the card stock. Be careful not to cover any slits not yet used.

The paper strips are held quite firmly in place during the weaving process and the strips do not usually need to be taped until the entire design has been completed except for the lattice weaving technique.

Lattice Weaving or Caning Technique

This technique weaves Papuela paper strips in a variety of patterns over a large square, circular or rectangular opening to produce a lattice design. Add Papuela tackies as you weave or decorate the lattice with embellishments or 3-D flowers and you will have created a beautiful project!

Key Points and General Instructions

The templates for the square and rectangle only have one half of the design on the template, you need to flip the template over to complete the other half of the design. To make this process easier, after taping the template to your card stock, draw in pencil the inside of the triangle to make the square or rectangle. Cut your weaving pattern around the edge. Remove the template, turn it over and then align the template again along the diagonal line. Place the template so that the diagonal line lies along that edge of the template. Tape the template in place and then cut you weaving pattern. Draw the remaining sides of the triangle. Remove your template and cut the rectangle or square with a ruler and hobby knife. If you wish you may cut it using the template as well.

You will note on each template there are short and long grooves. The short grooves are used for the horizontal and vertical strips of paper and the long grooves for the diagonal strips of paper. When weaving with the long needle, as you come up through the first hole immediately begin weaving (over and under) the strips already in place as indicated on the diagrams. Place the tip of your needle into the hole on the opposite side. Gently pull the paper strip through the entire pattern.

Prior to weaving a strip you may wish to slightly open the slit on the opposite side using your flat needle or a needle found on a piercing tool. This will allow the Papuela needle to slip through the desired slit easily.

Always complete the vertical and horizontal strips first followed by the diagonal strips.

To ensure a tight weaving design, tape the ends of the Papuela paper strips after each step i.e. tape ends after you have completed the vertical strips, then after the horizontal strips and finally after the diagonal strips.

For each of the shapes used in this book follow the diagram in order.

Finish the card by attaching a piece of card stock

Basic Materials Required

- Long Papuela needle (PU1004)
- Templates: PU0020 (rectangle); PU0022 (circle) and PU0023 (square).
- Circle cutter (optional)
- Other basic materials for Papuela

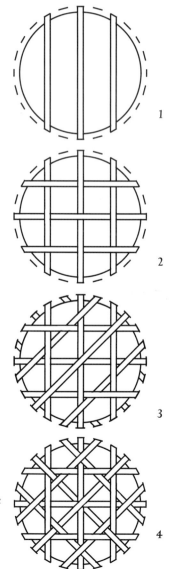

1

2

3

4

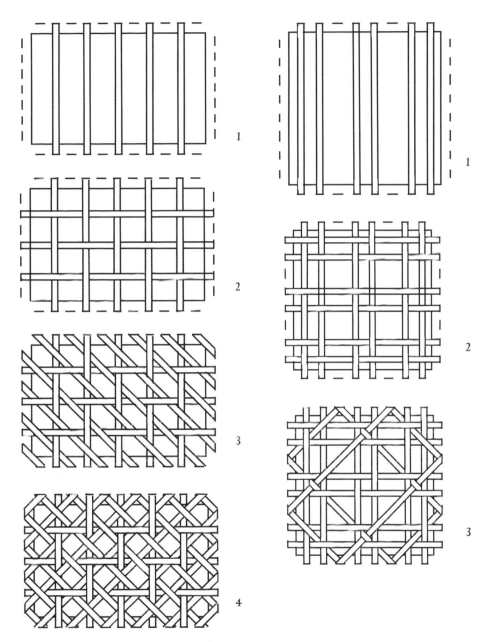

1

1

2

2

3

3

4

with the same window cut out of the center to the back to cover the weaving strips. The easiest way to create your cover sheet is to use the cut out card before you begin weaving as a template for your cover sheet. That is cut a piece of card stock to an appropriate size for your cover sheet, place it in position and then draw with a pencil the size of window you need. Cut the window out using a ruler and hobby knife or circle cutter.

General Instructions for Incire Paper Cutting

"Incire" paper cutting is another craft developed by Nellie Snellen of the Netherlands. This craft uses metal templates to cut patterns into paper and then folds parts of the design back onto itself to create a unique effect. Part of the paper has been cut thus allowing a background color to show through and enhance the design. If you use "Duo-Paper" which has one color printed on one side and another color printed on the other side of the paper and then if you use yet a different background color to show through the cut outs you have a three colored design!

Key Points

Use a **sharp** knife for cutting the designs. There is an Incire knife available that comes in the Incire Starter Kit or is sold separately. You may already have an X-acto knife or similar hobby knife that may also be used as long as the blade will fit through the pattern on the template. You may want to try a hobby knife with a snap off blade. Whenever the blade becomes dull, snap off the old blade with small pair of pliers) and you are ready to cut again.

Use a glass cutting mat. When cutting on glass the knife does not cut into the mat making it easier and ensuring clean cuts. (try using the glass from an old photo frame).

Basic Materials required

- Incire templates (see specific project instructions)
- Duo-paper (available in a variety of different colors and weights)
- Hobby knife (sharp)
- Cutting mat (IC1002)
- Cello-tape
- Folding and scoring tool (IC1001)

Always cut from the corner of the design down. For example, if you are cutting a triangular design cut from the top of the triangle down one side and then from the top down the other side. Cut the entire pattern on one side and then turn the template and cut the other side of the pattern. If you are cutting squares you must also cut from each corner out. This means that you need to move your template and paper frequently.

Move the knife from a 45 to 90 degree angle as you cut the pattern (or even a slightly greater angle than 90 degrees i.e. the knife blade facing upwards at the end of the cut). This technique will ensure you cut the entire length of the pattern.

Cut the entire design before you remove the template. Turn the template over to ensure that you have cut the entire pattern. Cut any missing areas.

Score the area to be folded with the small tip of the Incire Folding tool. A ruler may be used to ensure even scoring and thus even folding of large patterned areas.

Before folding, gently push the tip of the design to be folded from the back to the front using the pointed end of the folding tool this will allow you to slip the large end of the folding tool behind the area to be folded.

Instructions

Place the Incire metal template on top of your paper (place on the front side of the paper) and secure using Incire tape (a special tape that will hold your template securely to your paper but is easily removed) or cello-tape. You may also wish to tape the template to the cutting mat to ensure it does not move.

Cut all of the design that you wish to use (see above).

Turn the template and attached paper over to ensure you have not missed cutting any of the design.

Remove the template from the paper.

Score the areas to be folded on the front side of the paper.

Take the folding tool and fold over the parts of the design previously scored and rub over with the folding tool to ensure a firm crease.

Start at the bottom of the pattern row.

Attach the background colored sheet of paper.

Incire Punches

There are now Incire punches available in several sizes and designs. They are easy to use and create many unique projects. Use them on lightweight card stock, vellum or try them on any lightweight papers that you may have

Basic Materials required

■ Incire Punch
■ Lightweight duo punch paper or vellum
■ Scissors
■ Perga glue

Tips for using INCIRE punches

Once again duo paper allows you to create a multicolor effect however, using the punches on multicolored or patterned vellum is also beautiful. There is a large selection of special lightweight duo paper available for use with the Incire punches.

Folding and layering the different punched designs make accents, sometime you must also cut parts of the design to fold and layer (e.g. Butterflies).

The miniature Incire punches are used as little tags to enhance your designs. The miniature punched designs are not folded and thus do not require duo-colored paper.

General Instructions for Parchment Paper Craft

If you are about to try Parchment Paper Craft for the first time or have been enjoying the craft for a while we encourage you to study the following instructions carefully. For more detailed instructions or if you wish to pursue this craft further we recommend one of the following books: Pergamano Parchment Craft Basic Techniques (#9701), Parchment Craft (#9709), Magic Hobbies Parchment Craft (#MH10) or the Pergamano Instructional Video (#9220). It is probably best to try out the techniques a few times before you make your first card. The techniques you will use are: • Tracing patterns • Adding Color • Embossing • Perforating • Cutting • Using the Pergamano grid.

Tracing (copying the pattern)

The parchment paper is translucent which makes tracing the pattern easy. You will need a sheet of parchment paper that is about 1-2 cm larger than the actual card.

Tape the parchment paper to the pattern using cello-tape to ensure the pattern does not slip.

If you are making a folded design make sure that you position your pattern so you have enough parchment paper to fold over to make the back of the card.

Shake the Tinta ink well before starting, as the ink tends to settle. Stir from time to time using a plastic stir stick to ensure a consistent color.

Remove the pen nib from the end of the tracing pen, reverse and replace with the pen nib now showing. This storage space protects the pen nib from damage and should be used to store the pen nib.

Only dip the pen nib into the ink as far as the hole you see in the middle of the pen nib. This will ensure that only a small amount of ink is used at any one time. Tracing should be done lightly with thin lines. Do not press too hard on the tracing pen and keep the pen as upright as possible to generate thin lines. Please note that sometimes when the nib is new the ink will not flow easily because of an oily film left on from the manufacturing process. Rinse the nib under hot water, dry with paper towel and try again.

Trace pattern in Tinta ink. Most patterns are traced in white or gold ink however, any of the Tinta inks may be used to trace.

Basic Materials required
- Pergamano Parchment vellum (available in a variety of sizes and volumes)
- Tracing pen (1420)
- Perforating/piercing pad (1419)
- Embossing pad (1413)
- 2-needle tool or 2-needle split tool (1106 or 1125)
- Embossing tools [medium (1101), large (1102), and small ball (1107) and fine (1103)]

Before using the gold ink, stir the ink well using a plastic stir stick. Then with the stir stick, place a drop of gold ink onto the back of the pen nib, then trace. Some of the small dots shown on the patterns indicate areas that are to be perforated and these do not need to be copied on to the card (see perforating tips). The dotted fold lines of the card should be copied over with a white pencil crayon.

When you are finished tracing do not forget to rinse the tracing pen with water and then dry with a paper towel.

Adding Color with Dorso Crayons

Dorso crayons are available in 2 color combinations #1 (1440) and #2 (1442). Dorso crayons let you change the light gray parchment paper to any color that you choose. You may color a large area or a small area.

Dorso crayons are applied to the back of the parchment paper and must be done before perforating.

When using the Dorso crayons always ensure that they are at room temperature. Colors may be applied on top of one another, for example a little brown on top of green provides nice shading for leaves.

A drop of an essential oil (i.e. Lavender, rose, eucalyptus – found at bath and soap shops), lighter fluid or Dorso oil (1804) placed on a tissue can be used to spread color evenly for large areas.

To add shading to your Dorso colored areas use a fine embossing tool on top of the color and make fine lines close together. Make lines by either flowing from the outside edge to the center or from the center to outside edge

Unwanted pastel color can be removed with the Pergamano eraser (#1423) or by rubbing gently with a tissue that has had a drop of lighter fluid or essential oil added.

Embossing

The embossing tools are used on the back of the pattern thus raising the design on the front.

Pergamano parchment paper turns from light gray to satin white when it is embossed. If you are embossing a painted/inked area you will see the color become lighter.

Place your card design side down on an embossing pad (we recommend the deluxe embossing pad # 1413).

It is important to use the correct pressure when embossing. The pressure is different depending on which tool you are using:

Extra fine embossing tool: use only light pressure or you will go through the paper

Medium embossing tool: use slightly harder pressure

Large embossing tool: use much harder pressure

Try the tools out on a spare piece of paper – you need enough pressure to turn the paper white but not too much that the tool goes through the paper.

Always emboss lightly at first then go over the area again, using a little more pressure in the same direction.

For larger areas first apply pressure with the back end of the large embossing tool, then emboss again with the round tip end applying more pressure. Sometimes portions of the outline should be embossed with the fine embossing tool to give a neat overall effect.

Star embossing tool: is used from the back of the parchment paper on the hard side of your embossing pad (bottom). Place the star embossing tool on the paper and gently rotate it around at approximately a 30-degree angle. This motion should create the intended effect on the parchment paper.

Perforating

Place your traced and colored design on your pattern and perforate through the paper and pattern as indicated.

Perforating is usually done from the front of the design i.e. with the right side facing you.

Perforating may also be done from the back to have a raised design on the front (this will be specified in the project instructions).

Always make sure you work on a perforating pad.

Always hold the perforating pen straight up and down.

Dip your tool in Perga-soft (#1802) to make perforating easier.

Perforating may also be done lightly against a ruler to make a straight line.

To perforate edges use the 2-needle tool or 2-needle split tool. To ensure a neat perforated edge, try to evenly space the holes. This is done by placing the first needle of the 2-needle tool in the last hole each time.

Push out perforated edges on your perforating pad by gently pressing beside the perforated edge with your thumbnail.

For a neater edge, cut the perforations with scissors holding the scissors as described below.

When asked to push out small areas that are perforated, use scissors to get into small corners.

Cutting Perforations

Cutting is done using Pergamano scissors (#1132) or the Perga-Cutter (#1133). The Perga-Cutter cuts like scissors but works like tweezers. It is recommended for left-handed persons and persons with large hands or finger joint problems. The Perga-Cutter is held in your hand like a pen or pencil

Place perforated card on perforating pad to show up the perforations.

Hold the scissors with the curved end pointing down and towards you. Place the middle and index fingers into holes from the top (this may feel awkward but you will soon get used to it). The index finger grips and holds the scissors steady and the middle finger opens and shuts them – they need only to be opened about 1 mm. This will also ensure the tips of the scissors line up straight with the perforations.

Hold the scissors at a 45-degree angle and only use tips of scissors to cut.

Give a slight twist to the left with scissors when cutting to ensure a clean cut.

Using the Pergamano Grid

In this book the Pergamano Fine Mesh Grid (1461) is used. This grid is available separately or a small version (which is what was used to create the designs in this book) comes with the Enhanced Complete Kit available on the website. The grid allows you to create designs that involve many perforations very close together.

When using the grid place your parchment paper on top of the grid. The paper is translucent allowing you to see the grid pattern through the paper.

Perforating is done using the arrow tool (#1124) (also included in the Enhanced Complete Kit above).

When using the grid always complete the length of each row before moving to the row beneath or above. This allows the parchment paper to stretch appropriately and creates a much neater grid design.

Perforate in each hole, every other hole or whatever other patterns you wish to try.

General Instructions for Spirelli String Art

Spirelli is a form of string art that has been adapted for use with card making and scrap booking. Die cut designs are available in a variety of shapes or there are also Spirelli punches available in 3 different shapes with each shape having 3 sizes. The technique is fast and easy.

Key Points

Use any type of thread for Spirelli, however, metallic and rayon machine embroidery look the best.

You may alter the size of hole/space left in the center of the design by altering the number of points/petals that you skip when you begin.

You may layer different colored threads in one design. Start with the inner layer, this is the layer that you will skip the most points when you start, the next layer you skip less points and if you choose 3 layers you would then skip even less points at the beginning of the layer.

Basic Materials Required

- Spirelli shape (die cut or punched)
- Thread (Metallic or Rayon Machine embroidery thread)
- Cello-tape
- Scissors

Instructions

Choose the Spirelli die cut or punch design to use for your project.
Complete the decorations in the center first (i.e. embroidered or pierced design) before you begin. This is helpful as the size of your center decoration will

help you decide how many points to skip when you begin.

Tape your thread to the back of your Spirelli shape and then count the number of points (petals, scallops etc.) you wish to skip.

Wind the thread in the space between the points you desire, winding the thread around the back of the Spirelli shape coming up between the points to the **right** of where you started.

Now cross the thread over your previous thread and place in the space between the points to the **left** of the previous thread.

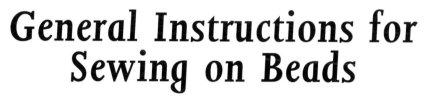

Wind the thread around the back of the Spirelli shape and come up between the points to the right of your last thread.

Repeat step #5 and #6 until you have completed your design.

Tape the end of the thread to the back of your Spirelli shape.

Use double sided tape or glue to attach your design to your project.

To create a 3-dimensional effect use small pieces of foam tape or blocks to attach your design, as this will raise it slightly off the page giving dimension.

General Instructions for Sewing on Beads

Beads are used throughout this book to accent the projects and attach vellum, 3-D flowers or Spirelli designs to cards.

Make a small hole in the vellum design, cardstock or both (if attaching a vellum design to the card stock) using Erica's very fine piercing tool. This tool creates a tiny hole that will be fully covered by the bead.

Basic Materials Required
- Erica's very fine piercing tool (EF0007)
- Needle
- Thread
- Beads
- Cello-tape

Thread a needle with a matching color of thread as the bead or to match the design. From the back pull the needle and thread through the hole and the design to be attached, push the design down against the hole. Now place a bead on the needle and move it down onto the thread. Take your needle and go back down through the same hole you came up through. (Do Not go down though the bead again). The bead will prevent the thread from coming out again and hold the design in place.

If you are attaching vellum or card stock to a card, just tape the thread to the

back of the card as it will eventually be covered by a cover sheet.
If you have several beads to attach then just run the thread between beads on the back of the card stock and tape the end again when you have finished.
If you are attaching a vellum design to vellum or 3-D flowers to vellum, then take your double strand of thread and create a small knot at the end. Cut off any excess thread. Follow the instructions in #3. When you have attached the bead then you need to once again knot the end. Try to have a long enough piece of thread that to tie a knot in the thread and then using Erica's very fine piercing tool, guide the knot to tighten below the initial knot. Tie a few knots in this manner then cut the thread close to the last knot. This process works well and you are unable to see the knot in your finished design.

Everything's Coming Up Daisies

The projects in this series use several techniques combining printed daisy vellum, embroidered daisies, punched daisies and beads into the beautiful cards, invitation, gift bag and lampshade!

Please refer to the following sets of General Instructions
• Parchment Paper Craft
• Embroidery on Paper
• Spirelli
• Incire Paper Cutting
• Sewing on beads

Daisy Lampshade (for use with a wine glass and tea light)
Photocopy the lampshade pattern provided on the photocopier enlarging it by 200%. Trace the lampshade pattern onto a piece of daisy parchment vellum using special Gold Tinta Ink or a gold gel pen.
Perforate around each of the scalloped edges with the 2-needle split tool and press out. Cut the non-scalloped ends of the vellum with a hobby knife and ruler or scissors.
Punch out 52 flowers using punch (IC0302). **Hint:** Cut a strip of vellum and then turn the punch upside down to ensure the vellum is placed correctly. Press down on the punch edges. Keep the center flower and discard the remaining scrap pieces of vellum.

Emboss the centers of the flowers lightly to make them curl slightly.
Pierce a hole in the center of each flower .
Pierce holes into the lampshade above and below the scalloped edges leaving 3 scallops between each flower.
Layer 3 punched flowers and attach to the lampshade with green beads using the holes just pierced. Knot each bead separately. *

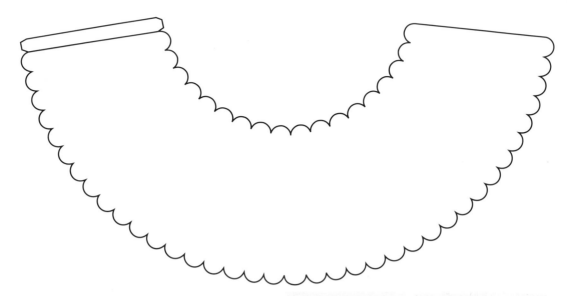

Use Perga glue to attach together the edges of the lampshade.

Use the lampshade over a wine glass. Place a small amount of water in the bottom of the wine glass and let the tea light float on the water.

Yellow Daisy Vellum Invitation

Cut out an 8 x 8 cm or 3 ³/₈" square in the center of a square yellow card.

Pierce the flower embroidery pattern provided in each corner of the card.

Embroider the pattern as indicated. *
Print your invitation information on the daisy parchment vellum paper. (Use a lighter shade of gray ink to print on the vellum). If you wish to print more information on the inside of the card it is best to do this first before you complete the embroidery. Attach the edges of the vellum invitation to the back of the square card using a glue stick or double-sided tape so that the invitation is seen through the cut out card.

Attach a piece of square yellow card

Materials Required

- Square and rectangle yellow cards
- Yellow card stock lightweight (sheet)
- White card stock (sheet)
- Spirelli circle die cuts in yellow and green (SP2501 & SP2503)
- Pergamano Parchment Vellum (Roses/Daisies 1620)
- Pergamano Two-needle split tool (1125)
- Pergamano medium embossing tool (1101)
- Special Gold Tinta Ink (1211) or gold gel pen
- Erica's multipurpose stencil (EF8018)
- Erica's multipurpose stencil (EF8009)
- Incire multiborder template (IC0021)
- Background stencil polka dot (AE1201)
- Incire punch (IC0302)
- 3-D foam blocks 3mm (AV8938)
- Light yellow and green (rayon) thread
- Yellow Ribbon
- Green beads

Tom and Mary Oskamp

Request the pleasure of your
company to celebrate their
40th Wedding Anniversary
Sunday the sixth of July
two thousand three
at three thirty in the afternoon
at their home

stock to hold the vellum in place and cover the threads from the embroidered designs.

Flower Gift Bag

Enlarge the gift bag pattern on the photocopier by 200%.

Trace the outline of the gift bag onto yellow card stock using a light box.

Cut out the gift bag using a ruler and hobby knife.

Emboss the lines as indicated from the back (EB) or from the front (EF). Use a ruler and the Pergamano medium embossing tool.

On the front and back areas of the bag pierce and embroider 2 corners of the flower pattern provided onto the front and back of the bag. *

Fold the bag into shape. Glue or use double-sided tape to put the bag together.

Punch out holes for the handles (open circles on the pattern).

Finish the bag by tying yellow ribbon through the holes and knotting on the inside.

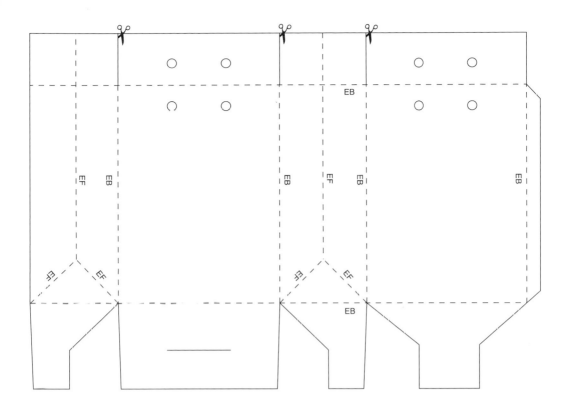

Circles of Flowers

Center and pierce the outer circle of flowers EF8018 into the front of a square card.

Pierce one set of leaves from the same stencil into the corners of the card.

Embroider the designs as indicated on the template. *

Pierce the grouping of 3 flowers from stencil EF8009 into the center of a die cut yellow Spirelli circle.

Embroider the 3 flowers and stem. *

Wind green thread around the Spirelli circle skipping 9 points. *

Attach a plain green Spirelli die cut circle into the center of the embroidered flower circle on the card.

Use 3-D foam tape to attach the yellow Spirelli die cut circle on top of the green circle. Off set the points so that the green points are visible between the yellow points.

Punch out 12 center flowers from Incire punch IC0302. See 'Hint' from the Daisy Lampshade instructions.

Emboss the centers of the flowers lightly to make them curl.

Pierce a hole in the center of each flower and in each corner of the card (above the leaves).

Layer 3 punched flowers and attach to the corners of the card using a green bead. *

25

Attach a piece of square yellow card stock to the inside to cover the threads and tape.

Polka Dot Gift Tag with Vellum border

Cut a rectangle card in half, or cut the size desired from a sheet of card stock. Emboss polka dots over the front of the card using background template AE1201.

Cut a 2.5-3 cm or 1-1/14 inch strip of daisy vellum. Cut the strip long enough to overlap at the back of the card, as this overlapping will cover the threads used to sew on the beads.

Place the Incire template IC021 on top of the vellum so that the pattern to be used is centered. *

Tape the vellum to the template (on the back) to ensure it does not move. Cut the number of repetitions required (8 reps for $^1/_2$ of a rectangle card). * Fold back the triangular designs.

Position your cut vellum on top of your card and tape in place. Pierce small holes just below the tip of each folded triangle through the vellum and the top of the card using Erica's very fine piercing tool.

Sew the beads in place. *

Fold the edges of the vellum strip to the inside of the card to cover the threads and attach with double-sided tape.

Flower Gift Card

Cut a 7x14 cm or 2 $^3/_4$ x 5" piece of yellow card stock (or use a plain yellow card from a set of miniature cards).

Cut a 6 cm or 2 $^3/_8$" square from white card stock.

Pierce the center flower and stems from the flower pattern on stencil EF8009. Pierce a hole in each corner of the white card.

Embroider the center flower, the stem and a frame around the edge. *

Punch out 6 center flowers using punch (IC0302).

Emboss the centers of the flowers lightly to make them curl slightly.

Pierce a hole in the center of each flower and in the white square card beside the embroidered flower.

Layer 3 punched flowers and attach to the card using a bead. *

Use double-sided tape to attach the small white square to the yellow card.

Friends are....

..flowers.....

..in life's garden!

A friend is a flower...

..in the garden of life!

Friends and Flowers

Your friends will enjoy receiving these cards that use different combinations of embroidery on paper, Ornare paper piercing, Papuela, Spirelli and 3-D designs.

Please refer to the following sets of General Instructions
• Papuela Paper Weaving
• Embroidery on Paper
• Ornare Paper Piercing
• Spirelli

Friends are...flowers in life's garden!

Place the upper left corner design on Papuela template PU0025 in the upper right corner of a brown rectangle card.
Cut the Papuela weaving design and window into upper right corner. *
Repeat steps 1 and 2 in the bottom left corner of the card.
Weave the designs in the 2 corners using 3mm or $^1/8$" rose-colored ribbon and the small Papuela needle. * For each of the 3 cross designs cross the ribbon of the center row over the window as shown in the example.
Print your message on a piece of ivory card stock spacing appropriately to allow for the embroidered flowers.
Cut out your message on an angle as shown approximately 6 cm or 2.5" wide at the top and 10.2 cm or 4" on the angle. Note the squared upper right and lower left corners.
Photocopy the pattern and pierce two flowers in each space between the printed words.
Embroider the flowers using rose-colored thread and light brown for the stems.
Attach a piece of lavender color card stock to the back of the weaving designs to hide the ribbon using double-sided tape.
Attach the saying with embroidered flowers evenly between the woven designs.

Materials Required
■ Ivory Rectangle and Square cards
■ Brown rectangle and square cards
■ Ivory card stock (sheet lightweight)
■ Lavender card stock (sheet lightweight)
■ Pergamano vellum Flower Fairies (1626)
■ Large embossing tool
■ Spirelli punch small flower (SP2606)
■ Weaving punch (PW002)
■ Papuela template (PU0025)
■ Ornare template (PR0536)
■ Wide and narrow rose-colored ribbon
■ Rose-colored thread
■ Light brown thread
■ White sheer ribbon
■ 3-D foam blocks (AV8938)
■ Perga-kit silicone glue (1411)

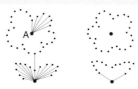

Embroidery, vellum and 3-D flowers

Cut a 10 x 11.5 cm or 4 x 4 $^1/_2$ " piece of light-weight lavender card stock.
Cut a 9 $^1/_2$ x 11 cm or 3 $^3/_4$ x 4 $^1/_2$ piece of flower fairy vellum.
Attach the vellum to the lavender card stock using Perga Glue or vellum tape.
Pick a few flowers on the vellum design that are situated appropriately on the
card to make 3-dimensional. Cut out 2-3 more of these flowers from the left
over vellum.
Gently emboss the flowers using the large embossing tool.
Layer these embossed flowers on top of the original flower attaching each
layer with Perga kit or silicone glue.
Punch slots on the left hand side of the design through which to weave sheer
$^1/_4$ " ribbon, using the weaving punch PW002.
Weave sheer white/ivory ribbon through the slits and tape to the back of the
lavender card stock.
Evenly space three single flower designs along the left hand side of ivory squa-
re card. Pierce each flower using the pattern provided. *
Embroider the flowers using rose-colored, and light brown threads.
Attach the lavender/vellum with 3-D flowers to the ivory square card.
Attach a piece of ivory card stock to the inside of the square card.

Spirelli and Embroidered Flowers

Punch out; 1 vellum, 3 ivory, and 2 lavender small flowers using Spirelli
punch SP2606.
Punch slits for weaving with PW002
into the center of the top and bottom
of an ivory rectangle card.
Cut narrow strips of vellum 8 mm or
$^5/_{16}$ " to weave through the slits at the
top and bottom. Attach the end on the
left hand side of the card with a small
amount of Perga glue. The right hand
side may be folded towards the inside
and taped in place.
Pierce the flower stems pattern (right)
just above the bottom woven edge of
the rectangle card. *
Embroider the stems using light brown
thread.
Attach the two lavender punched flowers just above the embroidered stems
on the right and left sides using double-sided tape. Attach the flower
punched from vellum above the stems
to become the center flower background.

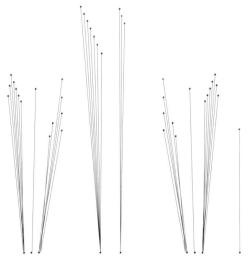

To create the two side flowers, take light brown thread and tape to the back of a Spirelli punched flower; skip 9 petals and complete the remainder of your Spirelli string art. *
For the next layer tape your rose-colored thread to the back of the design and repeat Spirelli string art skipping 7 petals. Tape the end of the thread to the back.
Repeat step 7 and 8 for the second flower.
The middle flower has three layers of threads. The first layer is rose-colored, skipping 10 petals; the second layer is light brown skipping 9 petals and the third layer is rose-colored thread skipping 7 petals.
Attach each of these Spirelli designs on top of the lavender and vellum punched flowers using 3mm foam blocks to give a 3-dimensional effect.
Attach a piece of ivory card stock to the inside of the card.

Vellum punched gift Card

Cut out a 9 x 6 cm or 3 $^1/_2$ x 2 $^3/_8$ "rectangle out of lavender card stock.
Cut out an 8 $^1/_2$ x 5 cm or 3 $^1/_4$ x 2" rectangle of ivory card stock.
Cut out a 7 $^1/_2$ x 4 $^1/_2$ cm or 3 x 1 $^3/_4$" rectangle out of the Pergamano vellum.
Punch out a small flower with Spirelli punch SP2606 at the left hand side of the vellum.
Attach the punched out vellum to the ivory rectangle using Perga glue.
In the center of the punched out Spirelli flower pierce only the flower head from the pattern provided.
Embroider the flower with rose-colored thread.
Attach the ivory rectangle to the lavender rectangle using double sided tape.
Punch/make a small hole into the tag and attach a piece of the sheer white/ivory ribbon.

A friend is a flower in the garden of life!

Print your message on a piece of ivory card stock so that you will be able to cut out a 7 x 7 cm or 2 $^3/_4$" square when you are finished. Put the message between the top and bottom of the square.
Using the same pattern as the previous card pierce a single flower into the center of the ivory square.
Embroider the design using rose-colored and light brown threads. *
Pierce a scalloped design into each corner of a brown rectangle card using Ornare template (PR0536). *
Attach a piece of 2.5 cm or 1" ribbon down the center of the card. Overlap the ribbon at the back to create a neat finish.
Attach the ivory square embroidered card and message to the center of the brown square card over the ribbon using double sided tape.

Black and White Cards

The cards in this series use the beautiful designs found on Erica's multipurpose stencils to create the look of printed card stock and then accents the cards with embroidery.

Please refer to the following set of General Instructions
• Embroidery on Paper

Black and White Tulip and Gift Cards

Cut an 11.5 x 11.5 cm or 4 $^1/_2$ x 4 $^1/_2$ " piece of square white card stock.
Align the outer corner design of stencil EF8009 in each corner of the white square and color in the design using a black gel pen.
Photocopy the square tulip pattern, place the design in the center of the card and pierce using Erica's very fine and coarse piercing tools. *
Embroider the tulips according to the pattern using black thread. Start first at C and embroider from C to the 5 dots placed in a v below. Then embroider from A to all of the holes forming a semi-circle below to form half of the tulip. Next embroider from B going into all of the holes as well (each hole will have been used twice) to create a cross over effect.
Attach the decorated white card stock to a black square card.

Gift Card

Cut a 16 x 8 or 3 $^1/_8$ x 6 " piece of black card stock and fold in half.
Cut a 7 x 7 cm or 2 $^3/_4$ x 2 $^3/_4$" square piece of white card stock.
Mark the center of each side of the white square card with a pencil.
Use the same design as used in the corners of the card above. Align the corner design of template EF8009 in the center of each side of the square white card.
Tape the card to the template and color in the design using a black gel pen.
Repeat step 4 for each side of the white square card. (see photograph)
Attach the decorated square white card stock to the black folded card.

Materials Required
- Black rectangle and square cards
- Black card stock (sheet)
- White card stock (sheet)
- Erica's Multipurpose Stencil (EF8011)
- Erica's Multipurpose Stencil (EF8009)
- Erica's Embossing Stencil (EF8001) Optional
- Black thread
- Black Gel Pen

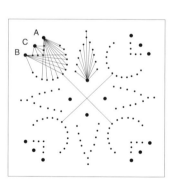

Doves and Hearts Card and Gift Card

Cut a 9.5 x 14 cm or 3 3/4 x 5 1/2 " rectangle out of white card stock.
Center stencil EF8011 on the white rectangle and tape the stencil to the card stock.
Pierce the oval frame using Erica's piercing tools. *
Color in the doves, hearts, and leaf designs on the inside of the pierced oval frame using a black gel pen.
Only outline the areas of the stencil that create an oval frame around the entire colored design (see photograph).
Only outline the areas of the stencil that create a diamond shaped frame around the center doves (see photograph).
Decorate each corner as desired. The example shown used corners from stencil EF8001 colored with a black gel pen.
Embroider the outer oval frame with a black rayon thread following the stencil pattern.
Attach the white card stock to a black rectangular card.

Gift Card

Cut a 16 x 8 cm or 3 1/8 x 6 1/4" piece of black card stock and fold in half.
Cut a 7 x 7 cm or 2 3/4 x 2 3/4 " square piece of white card stock.
Use stencil EF8011 and place the center doves and heart design in the center of the white square card. Tape the stencil in place and color the doves and hearts with a black gel pen.
Decorate the corners of the card using the design found on the outer layer of stencil EF8009 (see photograph). Color in each corner design with a black gel pen.
Attach the decorated white card stock to the black folded card.

Blue and White Cards

The blue and white themes of these cards remind me of the very popular Delft's blue pottery and tiles. This series also uses the beautiful designs found on Erica's multi-purpose stencils to create the look of printed card stock combined with embroidery on paper.

Please refer to the following set of General Instructions
• Embroidery on Paper

Blue Tulip Card and Gift Card

Cut a 9.5 x 14 cm or 3.75 x 5.5" rectangle out of white card stock.
In each corner color the design found on the middle corner of template

EF8009 using a blue gel pen. Tape the template in place and then color in the open areas of the template with the gel pen until the card stock is completely colored.

Center the tulip design in the middle of the rectangle and pierce the pattern using Erica's extra fine and coarse piercing tools. Embroider using blue rayon thread. * For the tulips start first at the middle upper large dot and embroider from the middle dot to the 5 dots placed in a v below. Then embroider from one of the larger dots to the right or left going into all of the holes forming a semi-circle below to form half of the tulip. Next embroider from the larger dot on the other side into all of the holes as well (each hole will have been used twice) to create a cross over effect.

Attach the white card stock to the blue rectangle card.

Materials Required
- Dark Blue rectangle and square cards
- Dark Blue card Stock (sheet)
- White card stock (sheet)
- Erica's Multipurpose Stencil (EF8009)
- Erica's Embossing Stencil (EF8002)
- Blue thread
- Blue Gel Pen

Gift Card

Cut a 16 x 8 cm or 3 ^{1}/8 x 6 ^{1}/4" piece of blue card stock and fold in half.

Cut a 7 x 7 cm or 2 ^{3}/4 x 2 ^{3}/4 " square piece of white card stock.

Mark the center of the white card stock with pencil.

Use the same design as used in the corners of the card above plus also use the leaves just below the design on the template. Evenly space 4 of these designs on the square of ivory card stock using the center of the card to create the design shown in the example (see photograph).

Align and color one design at a time.

Repeat above step three more times.

Attach the white card stock to the dark blue folded card.

Blue Square Tile Card and Matching Gift Card

Cut an 11.5 x 11.5 cm or 4 ^{1}/2 x 4 ^{1}/2 " piece of square white card stock.

Center the template on the square card and pierce the inner most design and the outer frame using Erica's fine and coarse piercing tools. Do not embroider at this time.

Using Erica's embossing stencil EF8002, center the square design (second layer from the inside or third from the outside) around the inner pierced design. Tape the template to the card stock and color in this square design using a blue gel pen.

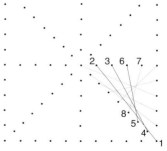

Decorate the corner using some of the leaf designs found in the center of template EF8009 as desired.
Embroider the pierced designs as indicated on the template and the center design as indicated in the attached diagram.
Attach the decorated white card stock to a dark blue square card.

Matching Gift Card

Cut a 16 x 8 cm or 3 $^1/_8$ x 6 $^1/_4$" piece of blue card stock and fold in half.
Cut a 7 x 7 cm or 2 $^3/_4$ x 2 $^3/_4$ " square piece of white card stock.
Using the template EF8009, align the template so that the center design is in the center of the white square card.
Pierce the design using Erica's fine piercing tool. Do not embroider at this time.
Using Erica's embossing stencil EF8002, center the square design (second layer from the inside or third from the outside) around the inner pierced design.
Tape the template to the card stock and color in this square design using a blue gel pen.
Embroider the pierced center design as indicated in the attached diagram.
Attach the decorated white card to dark blue folded card.

A Wedding Theme

The cards in this series combine the techniques of Incire with printed vellum and embroidery on paper to make beautiful wedding invitations, cards and accessories.

Please refer to the following sets of General Instructions
• Incire Paper Cutting
• Embroidery on Paper
• Sewing on beads

Wedding Invitation

Print your invitation information onto the Pergamano vellum (approximately 4 copies per page).
Cut your vellum to an appropriate size for your card stock.
* Note: In this card the triangle designs are folded in different directions merging in the corners.
Determine the size of each border you wish to make taking into account that the design merges in the corner. (i.e. in the bottom left hand corner there are only four triangle links while on the left hand side a full length border was made).
Make a small pencil dot in the place where you wish to begin and use this dot to align the template.
Use Incire Template IC0021 the 2nd pattern in from the left had side (vertical triangles).

Align the template on top of the vellum (right side up) Tape your vellum to the template. Cut the desired repetitions of the pattern. * Score the bottom edges of the triangle on the right side of the vellum and fold. * Repeat the above 6 steps for the remaining sides of the invitation. Position your cut out vellum on top of your card and tape in place. Pierce small holes just below the tip of each folded triangle through the vellum and the top of the card using Erica's very fine piercing tool (see photograph). Attach the vellum to the cards stock with beads. * Place a very small amount of Perga Glue or vellum tape in each of the corners so they will not curl.

Wedding Ring Card

Cut your vellum to an appropriate size for your card stock.
Place the Incire template IC0001 on top of the vellum so that it is centered.
Tape the vellum to the template (on the back) to ensure it does not move.
Cut the entire pattern on the template. *
Remove the vellum from the template.
Using a ruler and your hobby knife cut a straight line between each of the triangular cuts of the inner circle.
This will create an open circle in the center of your design.
Score the bottom of each of the triangles and fold back. * Place aside.
Center the wedding ring pattern on your card stock. Pierce the pattern into the card stock using Erica's very fine piercing tool. *
Follow the instructions on the pattern and embroider the wedding rings in gold thread (one strand).
Place the cut out vellum design on top of the card stock with embroidered rings showing through the center. Align the vellum frame and then tape to the top layer of your card stock.
Pierce a small hole into the tip of each folded back triangle of the outer circle and into the middle of each small triangle in the inner circle using Erica's very fine piercing tool.
Attach the vellum to the card with beads. * Glue the corners down with a small amount of Perga Glue or vellum tape.
Attach a piece of card stock on the inside of the card to cover the threads from the embroidery.

Materials required for all designs in this chapter
- Ivory Rectangle, square and miniature cards
- Ivory card stock sheets
- Pergamano Vellum (Daisy/ Rose Pack) (#1620)
- Background Template tulips (AE1204)
- Background template polka dots (AE1201)
- Incire Template, multi-border (IC0021)
- Incire Template, circle (IC0001)
- Perga Glue (1805)
- Pearl colored beads
- Gold Metallic Thread
- Ivory, Green and Peach colored thread
- Peach ribbon

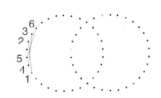

37

Small embossed tulip card

Cut a rectangle card in half, or cut the size desired from a sheet of card stock. Emboss scallops at the edge of the card using AE1201, then cut close to the embossed edge.

First cut the top of the card then the bottom layer.

Emboss tulips over the card using the background template AE1204.

Cut a 2.5-3 cm or 1-1/14 inch strip of daisy vellum. Cut the strip long enough to overlap at the back of the card, as this overlapping will cover the threads used to sew on the beads.

Place the Incire template IC021 on top of the vellum so that the pattern to be used is centered. *

Cut the number of repetitions required (8 reps for $1/2$ of a rectangle card). *

Score and fold back the cut designs.

Position your cut out vellum on top of your card and tape in place. Pierce small holes just below the tip of each folded triangle through the vellum and the top of the card using Erica's very fine piercing tool.

Sew the beads in place. *

Fold the edges of vellum strip to the inside of the card to cover the threads. Use Perga-glue or double sided tape to attach the inside vellum to the card.

Small embossed and embroidered gift tag

Punch out the center of the oval frame.

Emboss the entire gift tag using the background template AE1204.

Center the flower pattern for embroidery on the punched oval.

Pierce and embroider as indicated on the pattern. *

Place double-sided tape on the back of the embroidered design.

With the gift card closed place the embroidered design though the window in the card (this will align it correctly) and attach to the back of the card. Add a ribbon as desired.

Embossed or cut out vellum place cards and favor card

Cut 7.5 cm x 9 cm (3 x 3.5 inch) pieces of card stock for the place cards or 4 x 9 cm (1.5 x 3.5 inch) pieces for the favor cards.

Print the desired names on the vellum leaving enough space between the names to complete the place cards.

Favor cards: emboss the card with the AE1204, and then attach the vellum strip with ribbon.

Place Cards: Score a line in the center of the piece of card stock (lengthwise). Fold the card stock in half for the place cards.

Emboss the front of the place card with the AE1203 or two straight lines to frame the vellum strip.

Incire cut vellum place cards: Follow steps #4-8 for the small embossed Tulip card, to create the for the two triangular designs on each side of the name. The triangles on each side are folded back towards the edge of the card.

Plain vellum place cards: Attach the names to the place cards using double-sided vellum tape/film or Perga-Glue.

Jane Anne Brown
And
John James Smith

Request the pleasure of your
company to celebrate their
marriage
Saturday the first of September
two thousand three
At three thirty in the afternoon
St. James Cathedral
Toronto, Ontario

Reception to follow

John and Jane
September 1, 2003

Guest Name

Guest Name

Fun with Parchment and 3-D Flowers

The elegance of parchment vellum is highligh-ted in these examples that include wedding invitations and an inspirational saying. The layered 3-D flowers make perfect embellish-ments for that extra special look!

Please refer to the following sets of General Instructions
• Parchment Paper Craft
• Sewing on beads
• Papuela Paper Weaving

Blue Invitation

Print (using a shade of gray) your desired information onto Pergamano parchment vellum using an ink-jet or laser printer. Ensure that the information is spaced appropriately onto a 14.5 x 10 cm or 4 x 6" rectangle. You should get 4 invitations from one A4 sheet of Pergamano parch-ment vellum.

Using the border template EH1801, emboss the pattern into each side of the invitation (remember to emboss from the back so it is raised on the front).

Emboss the middle of the top and bottom edges using the swirls at the top or bottom of EH1804.

Use the fine mesh grid to fill in the bot-tom curves and top and bottom triangular shape between the swirls.

Perforate around the edges of the invita-tion with the two-needle or two-needle split tool.

Perforate around the inner edge of the two embossed swirls at the top and bottom with the two-needle split tool. Cut out with Pergamano scissors or press out.

Attach 2 flowers (made from two silver small flowers) to the bottom edge of the invitation with a blue bead. *

Materials Required
- Light Green, Light Blue, Yellow and Pink Rectangle Card stock
- Pergamano Parchment vel-lum (A4 sheets)
- 3-D Flowers (small and medium silver, blue, pink, green and white)
- Pergamano medium embos-sing tool (1101)
- Pergamano large embossing tool (1102)
- Pergamano small ball embossing tool (1107)
- Pergamano 2-needle split tool
- Pergamano Fine Mesh Grid (1461)
- Pergamano Arrow Tool (1124)
- Pergamano scissors (1132) *optional
- White Tinta Ink (1201) or white gel pen
- Background Template Polka Dot (AE1201)
- Border Templates (EH1801, EH1802, EH1804)
- Romantic embossing stencil (EC9676)
- Papuela needle (PU1001)
- Green, pink, blue, yellow seed beads
- White thread
- White sheer ribbon

Attach a single silver flower to each corner of the card stock with a blue bead. Attach the parchment vellum invitation to the card stock using sheer white ribbon. First cut two small slits into the card stock. Thread the ribbon into the Papuela needle and weave through the card stock and vellum (use the holes created from perforating out the swirls). Tie a bow and cut off excess ribbon.

Polka Dot Lampshade (for use with a wine glass and tea light)
Photocopy and enlarge by 200 % the lampshade pattern from the Chapter 1. Trace the lampshade pattern onto a piece of Pergamano parchment vellum using special White Tinta Ink or a white gel pen.
Emboss the entire lampshade with polka dots from AE1201. Maintain the pattern as you move the lampshade over the embossing template.
Perforate around each of the scalloped edges with the 2-needle split tool. Cut the non-scalloped ends of the vellum with a hobby knife and ruler.
Punch out 14 small white die-cut 3-D flowers.
Emboss the centers of the flowers lightly to make them curl.
Pierce a hole in the center of each flower.
Pierce holes into the lampshade above the bottom and below the top scalloped edges leaving 3 scallops between each hole.
Attach the flowers to the lampshade with pink beads using the holes just pierced. *
Use Perga glue to attach the edges of the lampshade together.

Use the lampshade over a wine glass. Place a small amount of water in the bottom of the wine glass and let the tea light float on the water.

Yellow Inspirational Card
Print desired information as in described for the Blue Invitation.
Emboss the top and bottom edges of the vellum with stencil EH1804. Emboss the outside edge of the stencil as well using the small ball embossing tool.
Emboss the middle of the side edges using the swirls at the top or bottom of stencil EH1804. Emboss the outside edge of the stencil using the small ball embossing tool.
Use the fine mesh grid to fill in the top and bottom designs and the triangular shape between the swirls on each side.
Perforate around the edges of the invitation with the two-needle or two-needle split tool.
Perforate around the inner edge of the three embossed petal shapes on the top and bottom designs with the 2-needle tool or 2-needle split tool. Cut out with Pergamano scissors.
Pierce holes in each corner of the vellum and through the card stock.
Attach one flower (make each flower from two medium and one small 3-D flower of blue, green pink, white) to each corner using beads. *
Attach the vellum to the rectangle yellow card by using Perga-glue under each 3-D flower.

Pink Invitation

Print desired information as in described for the Blue Invitation.

Using border template EH1802, emboss the pattern into each side of the invitation (remember to emboss from the back so it is raised on the front).

Emboss the middle of the top and bottom edges using the center design from EH1804.

Use the fine mesh grid to fill in the corners and top and bottom edge patterns.

Use the two-needle or two-needle split tool to perforate around the entire invitation.

Use the two-needle split tool to perforate around the inner edge of the two embossed scalloped designs on each side. Cut out with Pergamano scissors or press out.

Attach 2 flowers (made from one medium green and one small pink 3-D flower) to the bottom edge of the invitation with a yellow bead. *

Attach the parchment vellum invitation to the card stock using sheer white ribbon. First cut two small slits into the card stock. Thread the ribbon into the Papuela needle and weave through the card stock and vellum. Tie a bow and cut off excess ribbon.

Green Invitation

Print desired information as in described for the Blue Invitation.

Emboss the frame around the invitation using the romantic embossing stencil EC9676.

Fill in the areas between the angled embossed lines in the frame using the fine mesh grid and arrow tool. *

Perforate around the edges of the invitation with the 2-needle or two-needle split tool.

Use the two-needle tool to perforate the small areas between the lilies in the left upper corner and cut out with Pergamano scissors.

Attach 3 3-D flowers into all corners but the upper left (each flower is made of one medium green and one small blue 3-D flower) with a yellow bead.

Attach the parchment vellum to the card stock with sheer white ribbon. First cut two small slits in the upper part of the vellum frame and through the top layer of the green card. Using a Papuela needle thread the ribbon through the vellum and card stock. Tie a bow, and cut off excess ribbon.

Jane Anne Brown
And
John James Smith

Request the pleasure of your
company to celebrate their
marriage
Saturday the sixth of September
two thousand three
At three thirty in the afternoon
St. James Cathedral
Toronto, Ontario

Reception to follow

Autumn to winter, winter to spring,
Spring into summer, summer into fall----
So rolls the changing year, and so we change;
Motion so swift, we know not that we move.

--Dinah Mulock Craik

John James Smith
And
Jane Anne Brown

Request the pleasure of your
company to celebrate their
marriage
Saturday the first of September
two thousand three
At three thirty in the afternoon
St. James Cathedral
Toronto, Ontario

Reception to follow

John James Smith
And
Jane Anne Brown

Request the pleasure of your
company to celebrate their
marriage
Saturday the first of September
two thousand three
At three thirty in the afternoon
St. James Cathedral
Toronto, Ontario

Reception to follow

Sail Away!

My love for sailing inspired this chapter's red white and blue sailor theme. The projects combine techniques from parchment paper craft, embroidery on paper, Incire paper cutting and Spirelli. The picture frame matte highlights the many applications for these paper crafts!

Please refer to the following sets of General Instructions
• Parchment Paper Craft
• Embroidery on Paper
• Incire Paper Cutting
• Papuela Paper Weaving
• Sewing on Beads

Picture Frame Matte

Determine size of picture frame or matte you wish to make. In the example shown, the project was made to fit over an existing the matte of a standard 5" x 7" picture allowing the beveled edge of the matte to show. Cut the matte to be decorated to size.
Use Incire template IC0030 and determine the number of corner designs you wish to have in each corner. The example used three down each side of the matte with a common corner (see photograph). Align the template into the corner and tape in place. Cut the number of desired designs. *
Repeat step 2 for each corner.
Fold back the triangular designs. *
Pierce a hole using Erica's very fine piercing tool in the tip of each of the folded back designs and through the card stock underneath.
Sew beads in each of these pierced holes running the thread behind each design. The thread will show through to the front and becomes part of the matte. *
Determine the middle of each of the sides of the matte.
Using the second layer from the outside of stencil EF8009, pierce triangular designs for embroidery. The example used 3 for the width and 5 for the length.
Embroider the designs. * There are several

Materials Required
■ Dark blue card stock (sheets)
■ Dark blue rectangle card
■ White Spirelli oval die cut shape
■ Erica's Multipurpose Stencil (EF 8009)
■ Erica's Multipurpose Stencil (EF8014) optional
■ Background Stencil (AE 1208) optional
■ Incire Template (IC0030)
■ Pergamano parchment vellum (A4 sheet)
■ Pergamano fine mesh grid
■ Pergamano arrow tool
■ Pergamano flower tool
■ Pergamano 2-needle split tool
■ Pergamano medium embossing tool
■ Pergamano small ball embossing tool
■ Red, white and blue thread
■ Red beads
■ Red ribbon
■ White gel pen

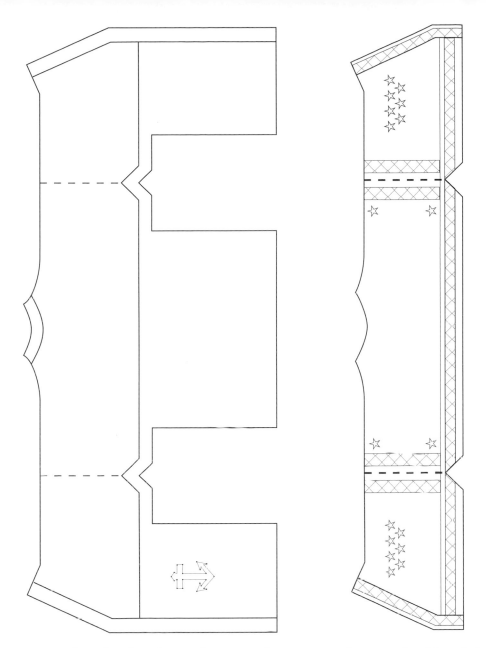

ways to embroider this design however the example shows embroidered designs in red thread with the triangular tip pointing to the outside of the matte
and then accented in the opposite direction with white thread.
Frame your picture.

Sailor Shirt
Photocopy the pattern provided for the sailor shirt and collar enlarging by 200%.
Cut out the shirt pattern and place on card stock. Trace around the pattern
(note fold lines on pattern). Cut 2 of these shirts as one will be used to finish
the card .

Using a white gel pen and ruler draw all of the solid lines of the pattern onto the blue shirt.

Score the fold lines using a ruler and medium embossing tool. Fold the card stock at the fold lines as indicated.

Place a sheet of Pergamano parchment vellum on top of the pattern for the collar. Tape in place. Place both pattern and vellum on top of an embossing pad.

Using the small ball embossing tool and ruler emboss first gently then more firmly all of the solid lines. Lightly emboss the fold line as well to make folding easier.

Complete the grid work as indicated on the pattern.

Optional: Emboss little stars in the center of each side of the front collar and in the corners of the back collar using either EF 8014 or AE1208.

Use the 2-needle split tool to perforate around all of the edges.

Fold and place around the shirt. Once the collar is aligned then attach the collar by sewing 3 red beads on each side of the front "V". Sew the back of the collar in place with beads in each corner. Once the placement of the beads is determined then pierce the holes through one of the corner grid holes through the card stock. *

On the front of the shirt, pierce and embroider the anchor in red thread. *

On the left hand side of the shirt and collar make a small single slit.

Use a piece of ribbon to make a tie by folding a strand of ribbon in half then make a single flat knot. A small piece of ribbon at the upper end will remain and slip this through the slit and glue in place with Perga glue.

Finish the card by attaching the second shirt layer to the inside to cover the threads.

Sailor Dress

Photocopy the pattern provided for the dress and ruffle enlarging by 200%. Photocopy but do not enlarge the collar pattern.

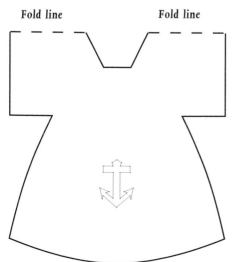

Fold line　　　　**Fold line**

Cut out the dress pattern from the photocopy and place on card stock. Trace around the pattern and then flip over to make the back of the dress (note fold line on pattern). Cut 2 of these full dresses, as the second layer will be used to finish the card.

Score the fold line using a ruler and medium embossing tool. Fold the card stock at the fold line as indicated.

Place a sheet of Pergamano parchment vellum on top of the pattern for the col-

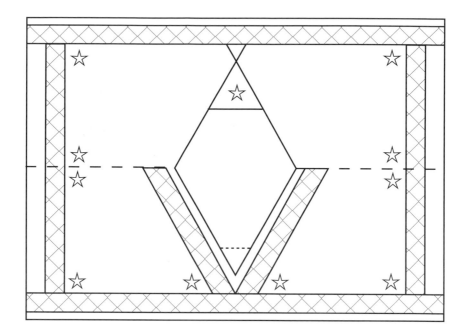

lar. Tape in place. Place both pattern and vellum on top of an embossing pad. Using the small ball embossing tool and ruler emboss first gently then more firmly all of the solid lines. Lightly emboss the fold line as well to make folding easier.

Complete the grid work as indicated on the pattern (hatched areas).*

Optional: Emboss little stars in the corners of the collar using either EF8014 or AE1208.

Use the 2-needle split tool to perforate around all of the outside edges and the inside edge of the collar. Gently press or cut out. *

Fold and place the collar over the dress. Once the collar is aligned then attach the collar by sewing 4 red beads on each side of the front "V". Sew the back of the collar in place by sewing a bead in each corner (in the grid work). Once the placement of the beads is determined then using one of the grid holes, pierce holes through the card stock. *

On the front of the dress, pierce the pattern for the anchor and embroider in red thread. *

Place a piece of parchment vellum on top of the dress ruffle pattern and emboss the solid lines using the small ball embossing tool on an embossing pad.

Perforate (from the back) with the flower tool as indicated on the pattern. Pierce the holes (from the front) for the beads in each of the scallops. *

Perforate around the edges of the ruffle using the 2-needle split tool and gently press out.

Place the ruffle in position on the front of the dress. Pierce though the holes already pierced in the scallops though the card stock. Attach the ruffle to the dress by sewing beads on to the ruffle using the already pierced holes. *

Repeat the above 3 steps for the back of the dress as well if desired.
Make two tiny slits into the card stock above the anchor. Weave a strand of red ribbon through these slits using the Papuela small needle and tie a bow. *
Finish the card by attaching the second dress layer to the inside to cover the threads.

Spirelli Sailboat card

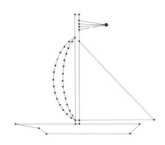

Pierce the sailboat pattern provided into the center of the Spirelli white oval.
Embroider the sailboat using red thread for the front sail and flag and blue thread for the back sail and boat. *
Complete 2 layers of Spirelli string art. For the first layer use blue thread and skip 8 points. The second layer use red thread and skip 5 points. *
Center the oval on the blue rectangle card. Pierce holes through the Spirelli oval and the front of the blue rectangle card which will be used to sew beads in place. Start with a hole at the top in the center of the oval then skip 2 points then place a hole in the next point. Continue in this pattern around the oval. Sew the oval to the card stock using 13 red beads in the pierced holes.
Pierce triangular designs for embroidery from the second layer from the outside of stencil EF8009. The example used 3 for each side of the card.
Embroider the designs. The example shows the pattern embroidered in red thread with the triangular tips pointing to the outside of the card and then accented in the opposite direction with white thread. *
Attach a piece of blue card stock over the threads on the inside of the card.

Go West!

The following Iris Folding designs are sure to please the cowboys and nature lovers among your friends and family. The folding designs are accented using Ornare paper piercing and Papuela paper weaving "tackies".

Moose

Cut a 9.5 x 14 cm or 3 3/4 x 5 1/2" rectangle out of ivory card stock.
Trace and cut out the moose.
Pierce the Ornare design as shown at the bottom of the card (see photograph) by using a small part of an outer corner design of template PR0559.
Cut 2.5 cm or 1" paper strips from 4 different colors. In the example shown the one leg of the moose is completed in light brown (#4) from IVP2033. The remaining three colors were chosen from IVP2038 and the antlers used one larger folded piece of rust color foil, the same color as used for #3.
Complete the moose. *

Materials Required

- Brown Rectangle Card stock:
- Ivory colored sheets of card stock
- Iris Folding Paper (IVP2038 and IVP2033)
- Tackies #2 (PU1006)
- Papuela Paper Strips (PU1104 or PU1108)
- Ornare Multi corner template (PR0559)
- Ornare Piercing Tool (PR0100)

Attach the brown 'crown' tackies in the corners of the card. Hold the tackie in place and using a hobby knife cut two slits into your card stock using the slits in the tackie as a guide. Do not cut the tackie. Attach the tackie using a light brown colored Papuela weaving strip and Papuela needle.* Attach your folded design to a brown rectangle card.

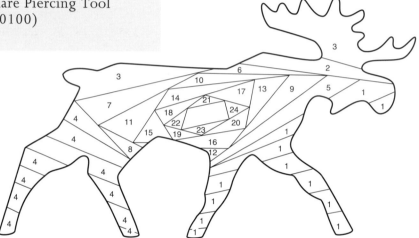

Western Hat

Cut a 9.5 x 14 cm or 3 $3/4$ x 5 $1/2$ " rectangle out of ivory card stock.
Trace and cut out the western hat. *
Cut 2.5 cm or 1" paper strips from 5 different colors. In the example shown, the brim of the hat used paper strips of all one color; light brown from IVP2033 and the rest of the hat used 4 colors from IVP2033.
Start with the brim of the hat. At the bottom of the hat begin placing folded paper strips with the folded edge at each line. When there is only a narrow piece of cardstock to attach the one end of the paper strip to, initially just tape the one end and then once there are several paper strips beside each other you may tape all of them down to the narrow edge. Do not let tape show through the other part of the hat.
**One paper strip on the brim of the hat needs to be double folded. This piece is marked with an asterisk. Instead of folding the paper in half…fold both edges in towards the center. Finish the rest of the brim in the usual manner. Complete the remainder of the hat. *

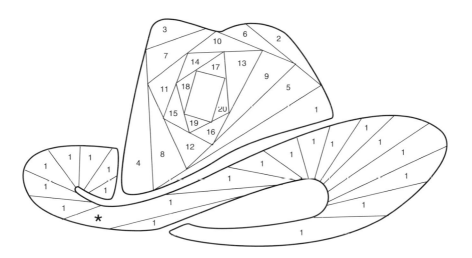

Pierce the design shown (part of an outer corner design) in each corner using Ornare template PR0559. *
Place brown colored 'star' tackies in the corners of the card. See instructions for the moose card.
Attach your folded design to a brown rectangle card.

Bear

Cut a 9.5 x 14 cm or 3 3/4 x 5 1/2 " rectangle out of ivory card stock.
Trace and cut out the bear.
Pierce the Ornare design as shown at the bottom of the card by using a small part of an outer corner design of template PR0559.
Cut 2.5 cm or 1" paper strips from 4 different colors. In the example shown the one leg of the bear is completed in the same color as #2. Three colors were chosen from IVP2038 and the light brown (#4) came from IVP2033.
Complete the bear. *
Attach the brown 'tree' tackies in the corners of the card as described for the moose card.
Finish the card as above.

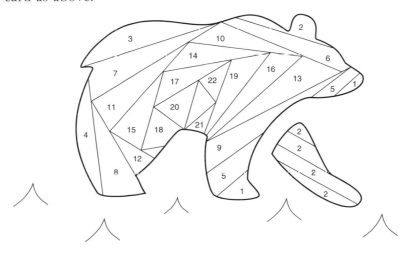

Parchment Paper and Spirelli Creations

Thanks to my mother Mary Oskamp for designing this beautiful series! These projects combine Parchment Paper craft with Spirelli string art and use beads and embroidery for accents. The black velvet wall plaques are decorated with circular creations that can also be used on cards. The black velvet wall plaques are available exclusively from Ecstasy Crafts Inc. all you have to do is add your creations!

Please refer to the following sets of General Instructions
• Parchment Paper Craft
• Embroidery on Paper
• Sewing on Beads
• Spirelli String Art

Instructions for Series Border

Trace outline with gold Tinta ink. *
Perforate with flower tool from back into scallops as shown in the pattern.
Emboss from the back with star embossing tool as shown in the pattern.
Emboss between traced outline edges of the scallops.
Perforate (from the front) around the entire edge using the two-needle tool or 2-needle split tool and cut or gently press out.
Add a tiny dot of gold ink into the center of each design created by the star embossing tool.

Luper Wall plaques

Complete border as per general instructions.
Trace inner circle according to pattern on a separate piece of parchment vellum.
Divide the circle into eighths according to pattern using white pencil (mark the back of the paper— these lines will eventually be erased). These lines are used to ensure the pattern is evenly spaced.
Starting at the center, begin embossing the outline of the different shapes according to pattern using the small-ball embossing tool.

Materials required

- Spirelli Punches small, medium and large flower (SP2606, SP2605, SP2604)
- Parchment Paper (1406)
- Sparkling Fantasy Parchment paper (1664)
- Luper #7 (1182)
- Medium embossing tool (1101)
- Small-ball embossing tool (1107)
- Flower perforating tool (1111)
- Star embossing tool (1122)
- 2-needle tool (1106) or 2-needle split tool (1125)
- Tinta Gold Ink (1211)
- Self-Stick Jewels (PR0304)
- Gold Metallic Thread
- Gold beads
- Wine colored beads
- Black velvet card stock
- Black Velvet Wall plaques
- Stickers (optional #325)
- Perga Glue

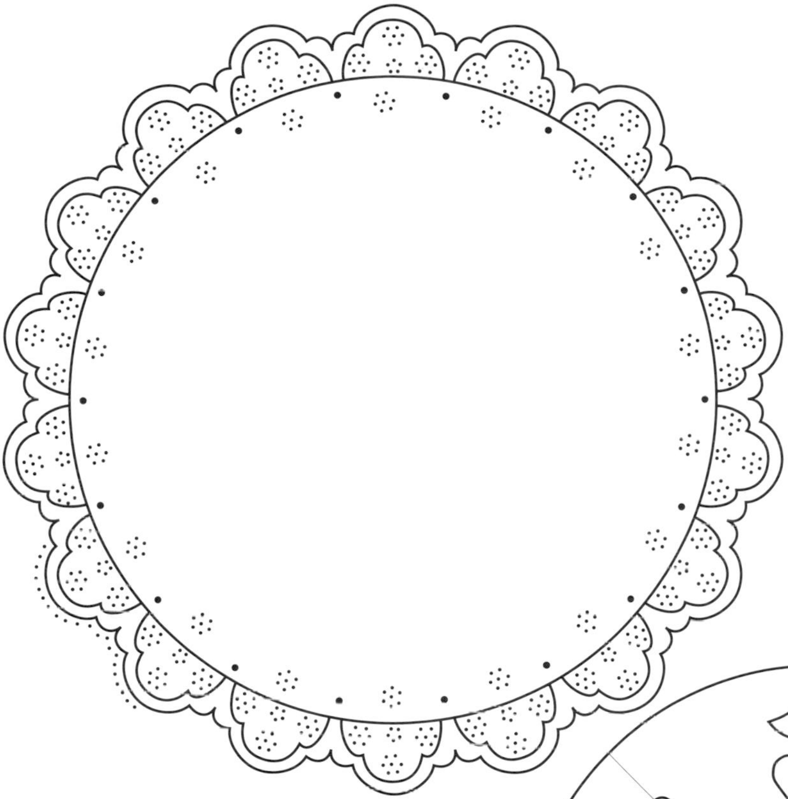

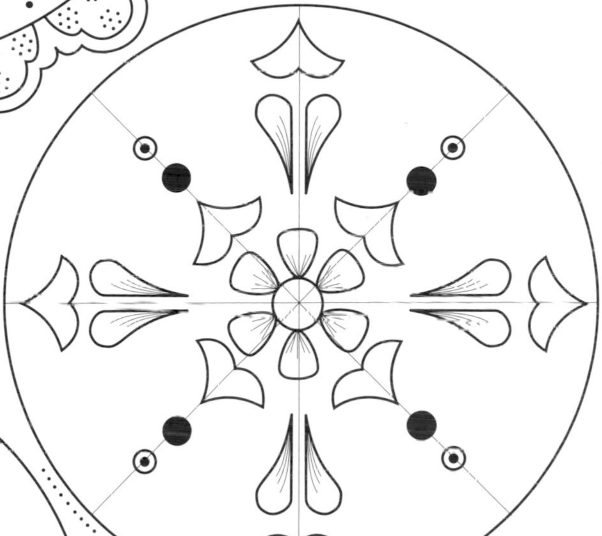

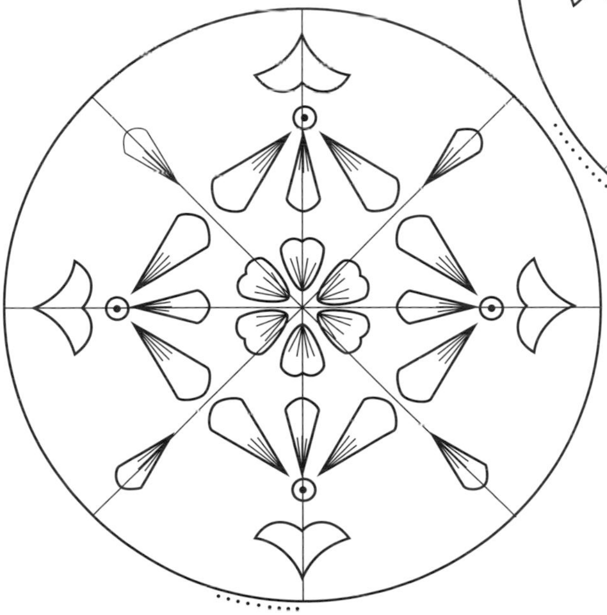

Emboss the small circles completely.
Emboss fine lines as indicated into the petals of the flowers and tear drop shapes.
Perforate from the back using the flower tool into each shape as indicated on the pattern.

Perforate around each of the petals using the 2-needle tool or 2-needle split tool, leaving the bottom of the petal attached to the center of the flower. Cut out the perforations using your Pergamano scissors or very gently press out.
Gently lift each petal to create a 3-D effect.
Place the inner circle on top of the background design in the desired position. Pierce 4 holes through inner layer and outer layer according to the pattern.
Sew the two layers together using gold beads each individually knotted to prevent thread from showing through. *
Glue entire design onto wall plaque using Perga-Glue. Perga Glue dries clear however, try to use small amounts of glue in strategic places to hide any traces.

Bookmark

Complete border as per general instructions above.
Emboss the design shown with Luper #7 and the small-ball embossing tool.
Emboss fine lines into tips of the Luper design using the small-ball embossing tool.
Perforate from the back using the flower tool as shown in pattern.
Punch out three small flowers SP2606 or trace the pattern provided and cut out.
Emboss the end of each petal using the star embossing tool (from the back).
Complete the Spirelli string with gold thread skipping 7 petals each time. *
Glue flowers onto bookmark and attach self-stick jewels into center of flower.

Spirelli Wall Plaque or Card

Complete border as per general instructions.

Punch out one of each size of the flowers SP2604, SP2605 and SP2606. You may also trace the patterns provided and cut out the designs.

The card uses all plain parchment flowers while the wall-plaque shows the largest flower and smallest flower punched out of Fantasy parchment in the dark purple shade.

Emboss the end of each petal using the star embossing tool (from the back). * The large flower needs 3 designs, the medium flower 2 and the small flower 1 according to the pattern.

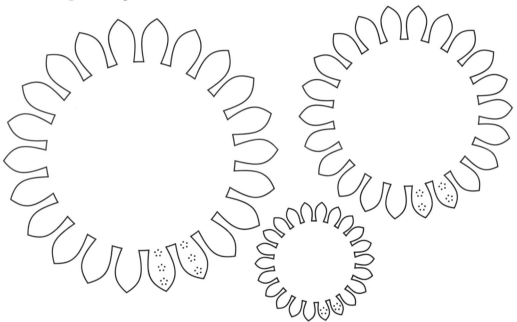

Add a tiny dot of gold ink into the center of each of the star embossing tool designs on the petals.

Complete the Spirelli string art with gold thread skipping 7 petals each time. * Optional: Place a small flower sticker onto Parchment paper, emboss each of the petals from the back and then cut out the flower. Glue this tiny flower into the center of the smallest flower.

Card

Pierce the pattern designs for embroidery into the corners of card.*
Embroider these designs using gold thread.
Place background design on top of card stock in the position desired.
Attach the three Spirelli flower shapes to the background by piercing a hole in the center of each of the flowers. Center the Spirelli

flowers on top of the background design and pierce through the background design and the top of the velvet card stock. Sew a bead through all layers. *
Pierce holes through the parchment paper and top layer of velvet card stock as shown on pattern by a single dot (between each of the perforated flowers) Attach the parchment design to the card stock by sewing gold beads into each of the holes pierced, taping the thread to the back of the velvet card stock. *
Add self stick jewels to the corners if desired.

Wall plaque
Attach the three Spirelli flower shapes to the background by piercing a hole in the center of each of the flowers. Center the Spirelli flowers on top of the background design and pierce through the background design. Sew a bead into the center through all layers.
Glue the background design with attached Spirelli flowers, to the velvet wall plaque using Perga-glue. *Place the Perga glue behind the area covered by the Spirelli flowers to prevent it from showing through on the front of the card. Glue gold beads in the position as indicated on the pattern (single dots) using Perga glue.

Fan Card
Complete border as per general instructions
Emboss areas according to pattern using Luper#7 and small-ball embossing tool.
Perforate into each of the Luper designs using flower tool as shown on pattern.
Emboss fine lines into tips of Luper design using the small-ball embossing tool.
Perforate (from the back) each gold line separating the fan sections using the two-needle tool (to ensure a straight line use a ruler as a guide). *
Pierce the pattern designs for embroidery into the corners of card stock. *
Embroider these designs using gold thread.
Place fan on top of card stock in position desired.

Pierce holes through the fan and top layer of velvet card stock as indicated on the pattern by a single dot.
Attach the fan to the card by sewing gold beads into the holes pierced. *
Place self-stick jewels or sew beads into the corners as desired.

Parchment Beaded Lampshade

Trace and cut the lampshade from purple fantasy parchment paper. Photocopy and enlarge the lampshade pattern by 121%.
Pierce the holes around the upper edge and the two sets of holes along the

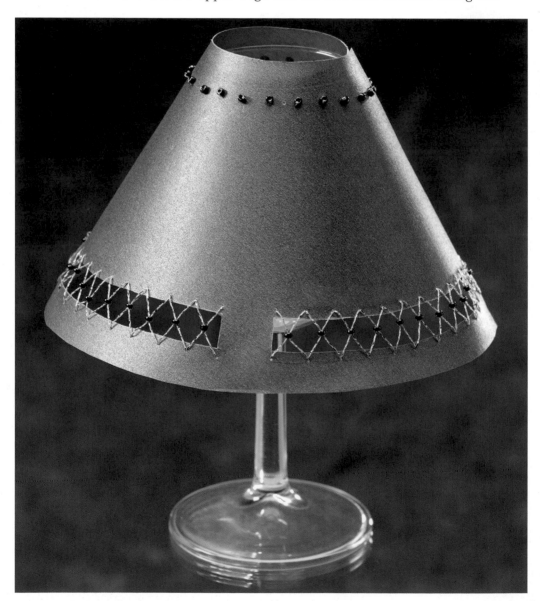

lower edge, using Erica's very fine piercing tool.

Cut the larger areas between the small hatched areas according to the pattern. The smaller areas that remain uncut give the lampshade strength. Embroider X's across the open areas with gold metallic thread. Follow the numbers on the pattern. Knot the thread at the back of the lampshade, come up through #1, place a bead on the thread, go down through #2, come up through #3, take the needle through the bead and then down through #4. Come up through #5 and place a bead on the thread then go down through #6. Come up through #7 go through the bead and then down through #8. Continue in this fashion until all of the open areas are filled with gold metallic X's and beads. Attach beads to the upper rim of pierced holes. *

Glue the two edges of the lampshade together with Perga glue.

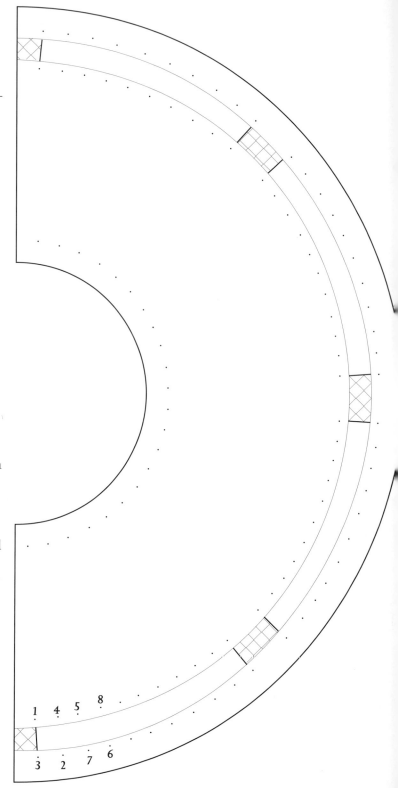

Designs in Green

The following cards all use papers found in one of the Iris Folding Paper packages. The techniques of Iris Folding, Incire, embroidery on paper, Ornare and Parchment Paper crafts are all used to create these unique designs in green!

Please refer to the following sets of General Instructions
- Iris Folding
- Parchment Paper Craft
- Embroidery on Paper
- Incire Paper Cutting
- Ornare Paper Piercing
- Sewing on beads

Golf Club

Cut a 9.5 cm x 14 cm or 3 $^3/_4$ x 5 $^1/_2$" rectangle out of ivory card stock.
Trace and cut out the head of the golf club. The handle and foot of the golf club are glued on top of the card stock. *Hint: Make an extra photocopy of the golf club pattern. Cut out the areas that have a pattern for folding and you will be left with the handle and foot of the golf club. Using this template (front side down), trace the design onto green foil. Cut the design out of the foil. Cut 2.5 cm or 1" paper strips from 4 different green colors (IVP2031). Complete the folding for the golf club. *
Print onto vellum the definition of golf or another saying you like. Cut to size. If you wish edge the vellum using the two-needle split tool. * Attach to the card using 4 beads. * Attach your folded design to a green rectangle card. In each corner of the ivory card stock pierce a corner design using stencil EF8012. Embroider with gold metallic thread and then complete the frame by adding gold sticker lines between the corners.

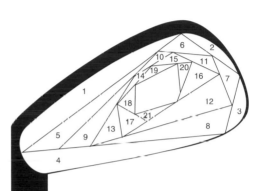

Materials Required
- Dark Green Square and Rectangle Cards
- Ivory colored card stock (sheet)
- Iris Folding Papers (IVP2031)
- Pergamano Parchment vellum
- Gold Foil
- Incire Template (IC0044)
- Incire mini punch (IC0503)
- Erica's multipurpose stencil (EF8012)
- Deco Stickers (#841)
- Green and Gold metallic thread
- Perga-glue

Fish

Cut a 9.5 cm x 14 cm or 3 3/4 x 5 1/2" rectangle out of ivory card stock.

Cut out the design for the fish using Incire template IC0044. * Cut the first 4 rows of the template then angle in to create a diamond shape. Cut the 4 designs at the end for the tail. You may wish to tape off the pattern on your template to avoid making any mistakes when cutting.

Punch out 20 triangular designs using Incire mini punch IC0053. The example used 3 different green colors of paper from IVP2031. Attach these triangular punched designs to the fish design by slipping the slit in the punched pieces over the cut out pattern in the card stock and fold the tip to the back of the card. Use the folding tool to ensure the tip lies as flat as possible.

Attach all of the fish scales to the design.

Pierce the 'water' design around the bottom of the fish using the pattern provided and Ornare piercing tool *

Place a piece of gold foil behind the design to show through the front.

Use stickers (wavy lines) to frame the fish.

Attach your design to a green rectangle card.

Place single gold sticker dots to the corners of the ivory card stock and the green card

Turtle

Cut a 9.5 cm x 14 cm or 3 3/4 x 5 1/2" rectangle out of ivory card stock.

Trace and cut out the turtle. *

Cut 2.5 cm or 1" paper strips from 4 different green colors (IVP 2031).

In the example shown the head, legs and tail of the turtle are completed using dark green foil in the same package of papers. Cover these areas first.

Use Iris Folding to complete the body of the turtle. *

Cut a single triangle pattern in each corner of the card using Incire template IC0044. *

Punch 4 triangular designs from green paper using the miniature punch IC0503.

Attach these triangular punched designs to the corners by slipping the slit in the punched de-

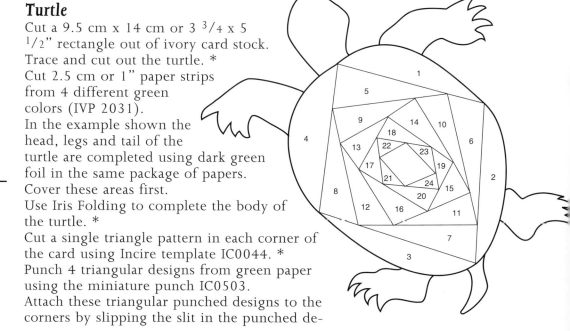

sign over the cut out pattern in the card stock and fold the tip to the back of the card. Use the folding tool to ensure the tip lies as flat as possible.
Attach your folded design to a dark green square card.

Christmas Tree

Cut a 9.5 cm x 14 cm or 3 3/4 x 5 1/2" rectangle out of ivory card stock.
Trace and cut out the Christmas tree.
Pierce the star patterns to embroider using stencil EF8012. * Place a star at the tip of each bough and at the top of the tree.
Embroider the stars using gold metallic thread. *
Cut 2.5 cm or 1" paper strips from 4 different green colors (IVP2031). The base and trunk of the tree are completed in green foil or the same as color #2.
Complete the Christmas tree according to the pattern. *
Attach your folded and embroidered design to a green rectangle card.
Decorate the green frame with wavy-line stickers.

A New Baby

Thanks to my mother, Mary Oskamp, for also designing an adorable baby series! This chapter combines the techniques of Parchment Paper Craft, Embroidery on Paper, and Ornare paper piercing to create these beautiful cards to commemorate that special baby's birthday!

Please refer to the following sets of General Instructions
• Parchment Paper Craft
• Embroidery on Paper
• Ornare Paper Piercing
• Sewing on beads

Ornare Baby Bib

Pierce the front of the bib card stock using the Pattern for layer A and the Ornare piercing tool. *
Center the template (PR0511) pattern which includes the 2 baby booties in the center of the bib and tape the template in place.
Pierce the pattern using the Ornare piercing tool.
Make two tiny little slits in the front of the card above the baby booties.
Use a small Papuela needle to weave the ribbon through the slits and tie a bow. *

Materials required
■ Square pink and blue cards
■ Bib pink and blue cards
■ Pergamano Parchment Vellum
■ Tracing pen (1420)
■ Tinta ink white (1201)
■ Medium Embossing Tool (#1101)
■ 2 Needle Split Tool (#1125)
■ Star Embossing Tool (#1122)
■ Pergamano Heart Tool (1116)
■ Pergamano Flower Tool (1111)
■ Dorso Crayons (fuchsia and blue Assortment #1-1440) Optional
■ Erica's Multipurpose Stencil (EF 8010)
■ Erica's Embossing stencil (EF8007)
■ Ornare Multi-Corner Template (PR0559)
■ Ornare Baby Template (PR0511)
■ Pink Self Stick Jewels (PR0306)
■ Blue Self Stick Jewels (PRO309)
■ Pink and blue ribbon 3mm or 1/8"
■ Pink and blue thread
■ Yellow thread
■ White beads
■ White pencil crayon
■ Foam tape (3mm) (AV8398)
■ Perga glue
■ Stickers "A Baby Boy" "A Baby Girl" (804)

A

Baby Diaper

Trace outline of diaper and inside card using Tinta white ink.
Mark folding lines (dotted line) and cutting lines (straight lines) with white pencil.
Dorso around outside edge of diaper with desired color. *
Perforate using the heart tool and flower tool (from the back) alternating tools into each scallop as shown
Emboss inside each of the pierced hearts using the medium embossing tool.
Emboss small flowers and 2 hearts from stencil EF8007 according to pattern.
Pierce center of each small flower from the back using the Pergamano flower tool.

Perforate with the flower or heart tool into each of the scallops of the inside card.
Pierce center heart on front of diaper using Erica's very fine piercing tool and embroider according to pattern. When embroidering on parchment paper it is best to start and finish off using a small knot instead of tape, as tape will show through the parchment.
Fold the diaper along fold lines and place tabs into cut slits.
Glue small ribbon bows on each side of diaper next to tab.
Emboss using EF8007 or EF8010 three hearts in each corner of square blue or pink square cards.

DESCRIPTION ON PAGE 61 ➤

golf /golf/ *n. & v.* —n. a
game played on a course set
in open country, in which a
small hard ball is driven with
clubs into a series of 18 or 9
holes with the fewest possible
strokes.

Attach a self-stick heart jewel into each corner as shown in example.
Attach diaper to card stock using double-sided tape or glue.
Add a sticker "A Baby Boy", or "A Baby Girl" to the inside card if desired.
Place inside card into diaper.

Baby Bibs

Baby bibs are shown in pink and blue. They each use the
same basic patterns however have different embroidered
designs in the center. Each bib has two layers of Pergamano
parchment paper attached to a bib shaped card (available in
6 pastel shades with envelopes). Pierce the
front of the bib card stock using the Pattern for
layer A and the Ornare piercing tool. *
Trace the outline of each of the remaining 2
bib layers onto parchment paper using Tinta
white ink.

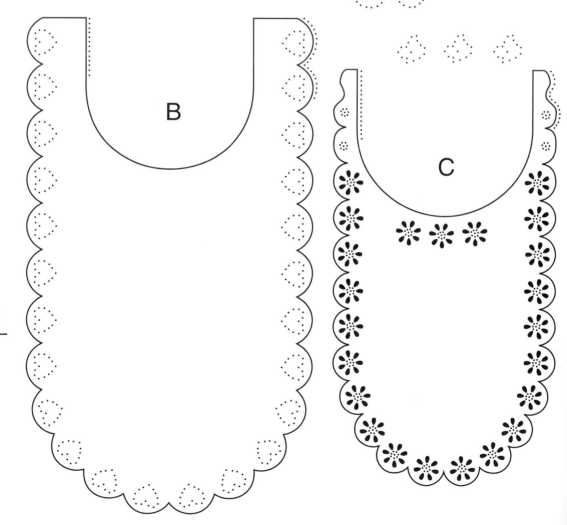

Layer B

Dorso the back of Layer B using the desired color (fuchsia or blue) Optional.
Perforate from back to front with the Pergamano Heart tool into each scallop
of Layer B
Emboss gently inside each heart using the medium embossing tool.
For pink bib card, pierce pattern for 3 small flowers just above the scalloped
edge at the bottom of the Layer using Erica's very fine piercing tool.
For blue bib card, attach 3 self-stick jewels just above the scalloped edge at the
bottom of the layer.
Sew a white bead into the center of each flower. *
Perforate around the entire outside edge of layer B using the two-needle split
tool and gently press out.

Layer C

Emboss a small flower into each of the scallops and under the neck line using
stencil EF8007.
Pierce the center of each flower from the back with the Pergamano flower tool
Perforate around the entire outside edge of layer C using the two-needle split
tool and gently press out. *
Pierce your desired pattern (baby carriage or sailboat) into center of layer C as
shown using Erica's very fine piercing tool. *
Embroider the design using desired color of thread.
Glue Layer B onto bib card stock at the shoulder area using Perga glue.
Glue Layer C onto Layer B once again at the shoulder area only.
Glue a ribbon bow to each side of the bib at the shoulder area using Perga
glue.

Layered Dress Card

This pattern uses a 3-D technique. Three layers A, B, and C are glued on the
basic dress pattern.
Trace onto parchment paper the dress outline as well as the circles on the sleeves using Tinta white ink (you may make the design as a card to be folded or
you may make a single dress to be attached to card stock).
Emboss using EF8010 stencil a polka dot into each scallop of the hem line
(remember embossing is done from the back making the polka dot raised on
the front).
On a separate piece of parchment paper trace each layer A, B & C.

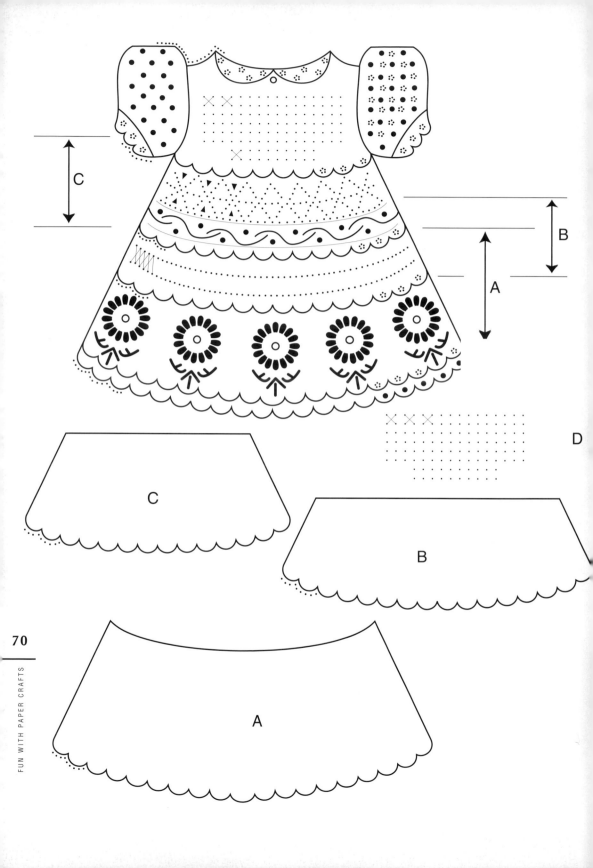

C

B

A

D

C

B

A

Layer A
Emboss flowers as shown on the pattern for layer A using stencil EF8010.
Emboss using the star embossing tool into each scallop of the pattern. *

Layer B
Emboss using the star embossing tool into each scallop of the pattern.
Perforate the pattern to embroider using stencil EF8010.
Embroider as shown using pink thread.

Layer C
Emboss using the star embossing tool into each scallop of the pattern.
Emboss pattern as shown using stencil EF8010.
Perforate (from back) the next pattern for the layer using stencil EF8010 and
Erica's very fine piercing tool.
Emboss small triangular areas between the pierced patterns.

Basic Dress Outline
Emboss using the star embossing tool into each scallop of the pattern on the
bottom of sleeve), between the circles and on the collar.
Emboss inside traced circles using the medium embossing tool.
Perforate pattern for embroidery using pattern provided (D) onto the bodice
Embroider x's as shown.
Perforate around the sleeves, the neckline and the scalloped edge of the bodice
using the 2-needle split tool (if you are making a folded card-perforate both
layers around the sleeves and neckline omitting the fold line and only the top
layer of the scalloped bodice edge).
Perforate along the scalloped edges of all layers (A, B, C and outline) using the
2-needle split tool and then gently press out. *
Cut straight edges along the sides of the dress with scissors or knife.
Glue or use foam tape to attach each layer onto the basic outline layer.
Add stick-on jewels into the center of the flowers on layer A as shown and add
a ribbon bow and jewel to the bodice just beneath the collar.
Glue the finished design onto a square pink card that has already been pierced
in the corners using the Ornare template PR0559. Use the 3 leaf like designs
from one of the outside corner choices. *

72

Flowers, Butterflies and Stars

The Incire punches are very versatile. In this chapter they are used with lightweight printed vellum to produce the beautiful flower, butterfly and star designs. The punched designs are also combined with the Papuela weaving technique for a custom look!

Please refer to the following sets of General Instructions
• Papuela
• Incire Paper Cutting
• Parchment Paper Craft
• Sewing on beads

Star Card

Place the Papuela template PU0021 close to the edge of the white square card and cut the weaving design into the card. Cut the rectangular window out of the card stock also. *
Emboss the remaining area of the card with stars using stencil AE1208.
Cut thin strips, 3mm or 5/16"of vellum with a ruler and hobby knife or paper cutter. Punch 6 center stars out of lavender lightweight card stock. (see Hint: Inspirational Gift Card). Cut small slits into the center of each star to make star "tackies". *
Weave the Papuela designs using the small Papuela needle and vellum paper strips. Take the paper strip across the opening for each center row of the design, add a star "tackie" and then continue weaving on the other side. *
Punch out 4 vellum stars from IC0303.
Evenly space two stars and glue to the white card.
Cut the remaining 2 stars from each star point in the center to the next space creating arrow tips.
Fold the inner arrow back and the outer arrow in towards the center.
Glue this design on top of the single layer already on the card aligning the center stars. Attach another piece of white card stock with the cut out window to the inside. *

Materials Required
■ White rectangle and square card stock
■ Lightweight white and lavender card stock
■ Incire Punch IC0303
■ Incire Punch IC0302
■ Incire Punch IC0301
■ Background Stencil Star (AE1208)
■ Background Stencil Polka Dot (AE1201)
■ Butterfly border Stencil (EE3401)
■ Papuela template (PU0021)
■ Pergamano Hydrangea vellum (1629)
■ Pergamano Parchment vellum
■ Pergamano medium embossing tool (1101)
■ Pergamano large embossing tool
■ Pergamano Flower Perforating tool (1111) (optional)
■ 2-needle split tool (1125)
■ Blue and clear beads
■ White thread

Inspirational Gift Card

Cut a white rectangle card in half.

Emboss the front of the card with polka dots using AE1201.

Print an inspirational saying onto Pergamano parchment vellum (use gray colored ink).

Emboss a frame around the saying using a ruler and small ball embossing tool on an embossing pad.

Perforate around the edges using the 2-needle split tool and press out. *

Perforate corners using the Pergamano flower tool if desired.

Cut a strip of lavender card stock to frame your saying.

Attach the vellum saying to the lavender card stock using blue beads in each corner.

Use double sided tape to attach the framed saying to the card.

Punch out 8 vellum flowers and 4 lavender flowers using punch IC0302.

Hint: Cut a strip of vellum (or card stock) and then turn the punch upside so you can tell if the vellum is placed correctly to punch out a center flower. Press down on the punch edges. Keep the center flower and discard the remaining pieces of vellum.

Attach the flowers to the white card using beads. *

Cover the threads with another piece of white card stock.

Flower Card

Using Background template AE1204, emboss 2 lines of scallops and cut approximately 2.5cm or 1" from the bottom of the card.

Cut 2 strips of lavender paper the same size 10.5 x 14.5 cm or 4 x 5 3/4".

Emboss one of the lavender strips with straight lines using AE1201 or AE1208.

Punch out 7 full flowers using punch IC0302. Save the center flowers.

Attach 3 single punched full flowers to the card as shown in the example.

Take two of the punched flowers and fold the end of the petals in toward the center.

Layer these on top the two outside vellum flowers.

Cut two punched flowers in half between the petals. Fold the two outside petals in on the adjacent petals (opening in center) of each half. Glue these 4 folded halves on top of the center flower creating a 3-D flower.

Punch out 5 more vellum, 3 lavender and 3 white center flowers using punch IC0302.

Pierce three holes in the lavender card stock and the white card where you wish to place the flowers.

Attach the flowers (1 white or lavender card stock layer followed by 2 vellum layers) to the lavender and white portions of the card using a clear bead.

Attach the second strip of lavender card stock to the first piece of lavender card stock over the threads used to attach the flowers.

Attach these two layers of lavender card stock to the white card covering the threads used to attach the flowers.

It is good to have an end to journey towards,
But it is the journey that matters in the end.

—Ursula K. LeGuin

Butterfly Card

Emboss a white rectangle card with polka dots using stencil AE1201.

Emboss a 4cm or 1 $\frac{3}{4}$" strip of lavender lightweight card stock with 3 butterflies and edge scallops using stencil EE3401 and a large embossing tool.

Cut the scalloped edge using the stencil and a hobby knife on a cutting mat.

Punch out 4 vellum and 2 white flowers using punch IC0302.

Pierce two holes in the lavender card stock where you wish to place the flowers.

Attach the flowers (1 white card stock layer followed by 2 vellum layers) to the card stock using a clear bead. *

Use double sided tape to attach the lavender embossed design to the bottom edge of the white rectangle card.

Punch out 2 flowers with IC0302 and 1 flower from IC0301.

Cut the punched designs out of the vellum. Cut each flower in half between the petals.

Fold the two outside petals toward the middle (leaving an opening in the middle) of each half. These are the two wings of the butterfly.

Now glue the two wings to the center flower/star design that was punched (the center punched flowers become the body of the butterfly),

Arrange the butterflies on the rectangle card and glue in place using Pergaglue.

Butterfly Gift Card

Cut a white rectangle card in half.

Emboss the front of the card with polka dots using AE1201 and a large embossing tool.

Using the pointed border design in AE1201 emboss and cut the front edge of the card.

Cut 2 strips of lavender paper the same size 7.5 x 10 cm or 3 x 4".

Emboss one of the lavender strips with straight lines using AE1201.

Punch out 4 vellum and 2 white center flowers using punch IC0302.

Pierce two holes in the lavender card stock where you wish to place the flowers.

Attach the flowers (1 white card stock layer followed by 2 vellum layers) to the card using a clear bead.

Attach the second strip of lavender card stock on the inside over the threads used to attach the flowers.

Attach these lavender strips to the back of the front of the white card.

Make two butterflies using IC0301 as described in the Butterfly card above.

Arrange the two butterflies on the card and glue in place.

Pastel Decorated Window Cards

These cards were made using 4 pastel shades of card-stock combining the techniques of Papuela, Ornare and 3-dimensional flowers. The heart and butterfly embellishments once again add a special touch!

Please refer to the following sets of General Instructions
- Papuela Paper Weaving
- Ornare Paper Piercing
- Sewing on Beads

Pink Card

Cut the weaving pattern from template PU0023 into a square pink card. Cut out the square window. *

Using the Papuela long needle weave steps 1 and 2 with pink weaving paper strips. Use green paper strips for steps 3 and 4. (* square instructions)

Optional. Cut a pink 0.8cm or 5/16" wide frame and glue on front over the weaving strip edge.

From the back of the card pierce the arrow corner design from template PR0536 in each corner. *

Punch out 3-D flowers, 4 small pink and 4 medium green.

Emboss the centers of the each flower using a large embossing tool.

Pierce a hole in the center of each flower, and in the 4 places where the flowers are attached (see the example). There are 4 small pink framed squares as shown where two green paper strips intersect. Pierce the center where the two green strips intersect.

Optional: Attach a heart embellishment.

Tape a double strand of thread from the top of the card. Bring the needle and thread to the front of the card through the hole pierced for the top flower. Attach 7-8 pink

Materials Required
- Pink and light green square cards
- Yellow and light blue rectangle cards
- Coordinating sheets of card stock
- Papuela Template-Square PU0023
- Papuela Template-Small circle: PU0027
- Papuela Template-Rectangle PU0020
- Papuela Template-Large Circle PU0022
- Papuela Paper strips: (PU1103)
- Long Papuela needle: (PU1004)
- Ornare Template PR0536
- Ornare Template PR0558
- 3-D flowers: Blue, Green and Pink (small, medium and large)
- Heart (KW3801) and Butterfly (KW3802) embellishments
- Small yellow beads and thread
- Coordinating Paper for framing optional (Patchwork Folding book- Pat 200)
- Perga Glue

beads to the thread. Take the needle and thread back around through the last bead to hold them in place. Take the thread through the ring on the embellishment and then back up through all of the beads. Put the needle back through the hole for top flower and tape to the top of the card again. The embellishment should be free to move however should hang nicely from the center of the card.

Attach the flowers to the card with beads. *

Finish the card. *

Yellow Card

Pierce the flower border from Ornare template PR0558 along the top and bottom edge of the card. *

Evenly space three circles from Papuela template PU0027 along the middle portion of the card. You may wish to lightly draw the circles in pencil on the card to ensure even spacing before cutting.

Cut each circle and weaving pattern separately. *

Weave the two outside circles following pattern A. Weave green strips for step 1 and pink for step 2.

Weave the center circle following pattern B. Weave green strips for step 1 and pink for step 2.

Optional: Cut small circle frames, 0.5 cm or 3/16" wide, using a circle cutter and glue on the front of the card over the weaving strips.

Punch out 3-D flowers: 5 small and 2 medium pink; 4 small and 1 medium green.

Emboss the centers of the each punched out flower using a large embossing tool.

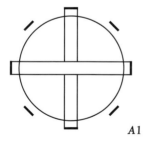

A1

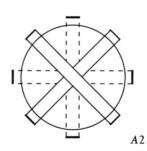

A2

Pierce a hole in the center of each 3-D flower, in the center of each pierced flower and in the center of each of the 3 circles as shown. Attach the flowers using beads. *

Finish the card. *

Light Green Card

Find the center of the card and pierce a hole using your Ornare piercing tool in the front layer.

Pierce the outer circle of Ornare template PR0536 lining up the center dot of the outer circle (in the center of the template) with the

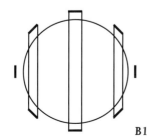

B1

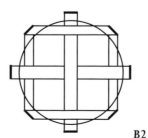

B2

pierced hole in the card. First pierce one half then turn the template over, realign and then pierce the second half. *

Center the circle of template PU022 in the center of the card and tape the card to the template. Cut the weaving pattern into the top layer of the card stock first * then cut the circle out using a hobby knife. You may also choose to use a circle cutter.

Weave green paper strips for steps 1 and 3 and blue paper strips for steps 2 and 4. (* see diagrams)

Punch out 3-D flowers, 5 small blue; 1 medium and large blue; 1 medium and 1 large green.

Emboss the centers of the each flower using a large embossing tool.

Pierce a hole in the center of each flower, in the center of the woven design (through the four paper strips), and in the four points shown in the circle, using Erica's very fine piercing tool.

Layer the center flower as follows from bottom to top: large blue, large green, medium blue, medium green, small blue and attach with beads. * The outside blue flowers are only single.

Finish the card. *

Optional: Cut a small circle frame, 0.5 cm or $3/16$ " wide, using a circle cutter and glue on the front of the card over the weaving strip edge.

Blue card

Cut the rectangle weaving pattern of template PU0020 into a blue card. Cut

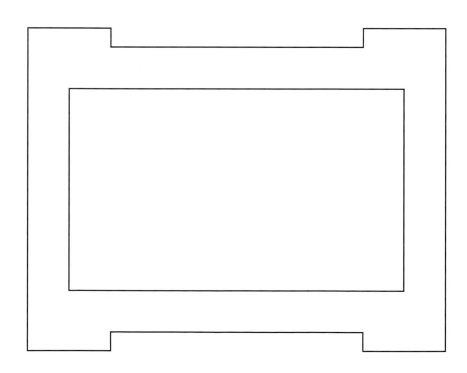

out the rectangle window. *

Using the Papuela long needle weave steps 1 and 2 with blue paper strips, and steps 3 and 4 with green paper strips. *

Optional: Attach a butterfly embellishment using a double strand of thread by sewing through a pierced hole in the top of the design. Follow instructions for adding an embellishment from the Pink Card.

Cut a fence frame out of coordinating blue paper according to the pattern shown and glue on top to cover the weaving strip edge.

Pierce the single ivy design from template PR0558 in each corner.

Punch out 3-D flowers, 8 small, 3 medium, and one large blue; 4 medium and 1 large green.

Emboss the centers of the each punched out flower using a large embossing tool.

Pierce holes into the front of the card for the 3 D flowers in a similar pattern as shown in the example (2 were through the weaving strips only and the remainder were through the card stock as well.

Attach the flowers to the card with beads. *

Finish the card. *

More Fun with Iris Folding

These designs combine several separate areas of Iris Folding to create these fun and colorful cards. They are accented with Papuela tackies, Ornare and embroidery on paper.

Please refer to the following sets of General Instructions
• Iris Folding
• Ornare Paper Piercing
• Embroidery on Paper
• Papuela Paper Weaving

Cactus

Cut a 9.5 x 14 cm or 3 3/4 x 5 1/2" rectangle out of ivory card stock.

Trace and cut out the cactus.

Cut 2.5 cm or 1" paper strips from 4 different colors for the main part of the cactus and 4 colors (2 the same as the main cactus and 2 different) for the side arms of the cactus. The flower required a single piece of yellow paper.

Pierce the 'grass' pattern at the bottom of

Materials Required
- Dark Green, Black and Dark Blue Rectangle Cards
- Ivory colored card stock sheet
- Black card stock lightweight sheet
- Iris Folding Papers (IVP2032, IVP2034, IVP2037, IVP2033)
- Papuela Paper strips (PU1101, PU1102)
- Tackies #1 and #2 (PU1005 & PU1006)
- Erica's Multipurpose Stencil (EF8012)
- Deco Stickers (#841)
- Black Thread
- Circle Cutter (optional)

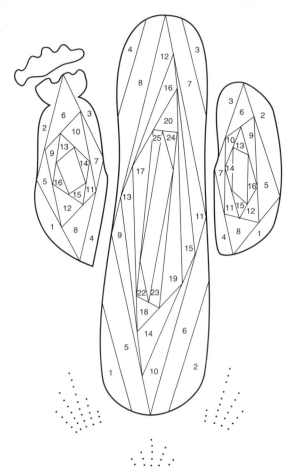

the cactus using the Ornare tool. * Complete the folding for the 2 side arms of the cactus first then the center of the cactus. * In the example, the 2 side arms of the cactus use the same colored paper strips however they are arranged to mirror each other. ** Hint: When there is only a narrow piece of cardstock to attach the one end of the paper strip to, initially just tape the one end and then once there are several paper strips beside each other you may tape all of them down to the narrow edge. You will need to trim the width of the paper strip to fit. Do not let tape show through any other parts of the design.

Attach the 'green flower' tackies in the corners of the card. Hold the tackie in place and using a hobby knife cut two

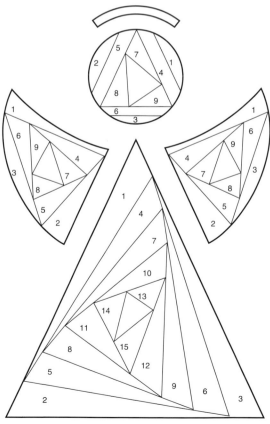

slits into your card stock using the slits in the tackie as a guide. Do not cut the tackie. Attach the tackie using a yellow Papuela weaving strip and Papuela needle. *

Attach your folded design to a dark green rectangle card.

Angel

Cut a 9.5 x 14 cm or 3 3/4 x 5 1/2" rectangle out of ivory card stock. Trace and cut out the angel. You may want to use a circle cutter for the angel's head.

Cut 2.5 cm or 1" paper strips from 3 different colors for all parts of the angel (IVP2037)

Complete the folding for the 2 arms of the angel first then the center of

the angel and finally the head. * In the example, the 2 arms of the angel use the same color paper strips however they are arranged to mirror each other. See Hint from Cactus card.

Use a piece of holographic paper or ribbon for the halo.

Attach the pink 'heart' tackies in the corners of the card as described for the cactus card, using a dark blue Papuela paper strip.

Attach your folded design to a blue rectangle card

Roadster

Cut a 9.5 x 14 cm or 3 3/4 x 5 1/2" rectangle out of ivory card stock.

Trace and cut out the body of the car and two inner circles of the wheels.

Cut out the frame of the car from black card stock. **Hint: Make an extra photocopy of the car pattern. Cut out the areas that have a pattern for folding and you will be left with the frame. Use this photocopied frame as a template to trace onto black card stock and cut out. If you have a circle cutter you may wish to cut out the frame without the wheel frames and then make two wheel frames using a circle cutter.

Cut 2.5 cm or 1" paper strips from 4 different colors. In the example shown the body of the car used 3 colors from IVP2034 while each of the wheels used only 2 additional colors that are alternated from IVP2034.

Complete the body of the car and the two wheels. *

Glue the black car frame on top of the ivory cardstock in the appropriate place.

Pierce and embroider a corner design in each corner from EF8012. *

Complete embroidery (from center hole out to each hole) in black thread.

Place gold line stickers (841) between the embroidered corners to frame the card.

Attach your folded design to a black rectangle card.

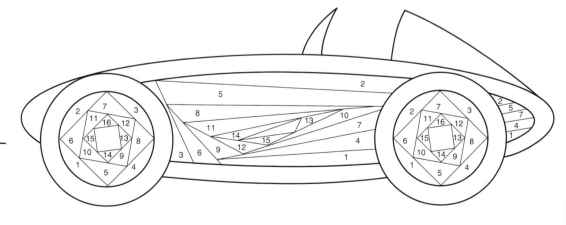

Let it Snow!

These blue and ivory Christmas cards are just begging for snow! The snowman and star cards are cut with an Incire template while the Christmas tree cards are also cut with a shadow template. The embroidered trees and stars glisten in an iridescent thread mimicking snow on a moon lit night!

Please refer to the following sets of General Instructions
• Parchment Paper Craft
• Embroidery on Paper
• Incire Paper Cutting

Snowman card

Cut a 9.5 x 14 cm or 3 ³/4 x 5 ¹/2" rectangle out of dark blue and ivory duo paper.
Evenly space the two snowman designs IC0042 on the duo paper.
Cut each snowman design separately. *
Score and fold back the 2 star layers starting from the outside layer moving in. Tuck the layers under the tabs (the tabs are not folded back).
Punch a star design into the middle of each side of the duo paper using border punch AP2002. Save the punched out stars and glue 1 into each corner with Perga glue.
Attach your Incire design to a dark blue rectangle card.

Star card

Cut a 9.5 x 14 cm or 3 ³/4 x 5 ¹/2" rectangle out of dark blue and ivory duo paper.
Evenly space the two star designs on the duo paper IC0042.
Cut each star design separately. *
Score and fold back the 3 star layers starting from the outside layer moving in. Tuck the layers under the tabs (the tabs are cut but not folded back).
Punch a star design into the middle of each side of the duo paper using border punch AP2002. Save the punched out stars and glue 1 into each corner with Perga glue.
Attach your Incire cut design to a dark blue rectangle card.

Materials Required
■ Blue rectangle and square cards
■ Incire Duo Paper navy blue and white (IC3017)
■ Pergamano Parchment vellum blue (1664)
■ Pergamano medium embossing tool (1101)
■ Pergamano Fine Mesh Grid (1461)
■ Pergamano Arrow Tool (1124)
■ Corner embossing stencil (EH1805)
■ Erica's multipurpose stencil (EF8012)
■ Erica's multipurpose stencil (EF8014)
■ Incire Template (IC0042)
■ Shadow Template (MM0212)
■ Border punch AP2002 (stars)
■ Border Punch AP2013 (Christmas scene)
■ Green and iridescent metallic thread
■ Perga Glue

Snowman Gift Card

Cut out a 6.7 x 9.5 cm or 2 3/4 x 3 3/4" piece of blue and ivory duo paper.
Cut out one snowman design IC0042 in the center of the card. *
Punch out 2 Christmas scene designs using border punch AP2013 at the bottom of the card and 2 star designs AP2002 at the top of the card.
Attach your Incire cut design to one half of a dark blue rectangle card.

Christmas tree card

Cut a 9.5 x 14 cm or 3 3/4 x 5 1/2" rectangle out of ivory card stock.
Cut out the Christmas tree designs from the shadow template MM0212 using a hobby knife and a glass cutting mat.
In each corner of the ivory card, pierce one small square from the center frame on the EF8014 stencil. *
Embroider the corner designs using green metallic thread according to the stencil pattern.
Place the ivory cut out card on top of a blue rectangle card and determine where to place the embroidered Christmas tree and stars. Pierce the Christmas tree from stencil EF8012 and the small and larger stars from the stencil EF8014. *
Embroider the designs on the blue card using green or an iridescent metallic thread.
Attach your cut design to the embroidered dark blue rectangle card.
Finish the card by attaching a cover sheet to the inside of the card.

Square Christmas tree card

Cut out an 11.5 cm or 4 1/2" square from ivory card stock.
See Step #2 from the Christmas tree card above, however only cut out the bottom three Christmas trees.
Place the ivory cut out card on top of a blue rectangle card and determine where to place the Christmas tree and stars. Pierce the Christmas tree the stencil EF8012 and the small and larger stars from the stencil EF8014. *
Punch out Christmas trees from blue card stock or paper using the border punch AP2013.
Glue the punched out Christmas trees in the corners of the card.
Attach your cut design to the embroidered dark blue square card.
Finish the card by attaching another cover sheet to the inside of the card.

Gift bag

Enlarge the gift bag pattern from Chapter 1 on the photocopier by 200%.
Trace the outline of the gift bag onto Pergamano fantasy blue parchment paper.
Cut out the gift bag using a ruler and hobby knife.
Emboss the lines as indicated from the back (EB) or from the front (EF). Use a ruler and a medium embossing tool.
On the front and back areas of the bag emboss the design from stencil (EH1805). Emboss from the back placing a design at the top and bottom of

the bag. Fill in the triangular area in the middle of the design using the fine mesh grid and arrow tool. *

In the middle of the bag pierce a Christmas tree EF8012 and a small star EF8014. *

Embroider the star and Christmas tree in green metallic thread.

Fold the bag into shape. Glue the bag together using Perga Glue or double sided tape.

Punch out holes for the handles (see circles on pattern).

Finish the bag by tying a ribbon through the holes and knot on the inside.

Christmas in Red and Green

These cards are made in the traditional Christmas colors of red and green combining Spirelli, embroidery, Ornare, and Papuela. They will be sure to delight their receivers and you may even suggest framing them so that they will be enjoyed season after season!

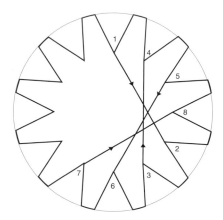

Please refer to the following sets of General Instructions

• Papuela Paper Weaving
• Embroidery on Paper
• Incire Paper Cutting
• Sewing on Beads

Red and Green cards with Gold ribbon

Pierce the Christmas tree or angel design EF8012 in the center of a green or red Spirelli circle. *

Materials Required

■ Red and green square card stock
■ Red and green Spirelli circles (SP2502)
■ Erica's Multipurpose Stencil Starlight (EF8012)
■ Erica's Multipurpose Stencil New Christmas (EF8020)
■ Ornare Template (PR0536)
■ Papuela Template (PU0021)
■ Paper strips (PU 1105)
■ Papuela Tackies (PU1006)
■ Gold Stickers (841)
■ Gold Star stickers (853)
■ Red gold and green thread
■ Gold ribbon and gold beads
■ Foam tape blocks (3mm) (AV8938)

Embroider the designs using gold metallic thread.
Complete the Spirelli string art in gold metallic thread skipping 9 points. *
Pierce the corner designs using EF8012 stencil and embroider in gold metallic thread.
Place straight gold line stickers (841) between the embroidered corners to create a frame.
Place tiny gold sticker dots (841) on each point of the Spirelli design.
Place a piece of gold ribbon in the center of the card, overlapping to the back.
Attach to the back and the middle of the front (where the Spirelli design will come) using double sided tape.
Attach the Spirelli design on top of the ribbon using double-sided tape.
Attach another piece of card stock on the inside to cover the treads and ribbon.

Spirelli Star Card
Find the center of the card and pierce a hole using the Ornare piercing tool.
Pierce the inner circle of Ornare template PR0536 lining up the center dot of the inner circle (in the center of the template) with the pierced hole in the card. First pierce one half then turn the template over, realign and then pierce the second half. *
Pierce the star design EF8020 into a green Spirelli circle. Embroider the star as indicated on the stencil. The example shown used gold thread for the inner part of the star and the outer part of the star was embroidered in red metallic thread. *
Complete the Spirelli string art using red metallic thread skipping 7 points. *
Place tiny gold sticker dots (841) on each point of the Spirelli design. Place tiny gold sticker dots (841) on each point of a red Spirelli design to be used as background.
Place tiny star stickers (853) around the pierced design.
Pierce 3 stars from EF8020 stencil in each corner and embroider using gold thread.
Attach the red Spirelli circle in the center of the card using double-sided tape.
Attach the green Spirelli plus embroidery design on top of the red circle, offsetting to allow the red points to show through the green using foam tape blocks (optional). The foam blocks create a 3 dimensional effect.

Red with Green Christmas Trees
Place the Papuela template PU0021 close to the edge of the red square card and cut the weaving design into the card. Cut the thin rectangle out of the card stock using the template. *
Weave the Papuela designs using the small Papuela needle and green paper strips. For each center row of the designs take the paper strip across the window to the other side. First add a green tree tackie in the window then continue the weaving pattern on the opposite side. *
In the remaining space on the card evenly space three Christmas trees from EF8012.

Pierce the designs and embroider according to the stencil in green metallic thread. *
Pierce the two corner designs from EF8012 and embroider in green metallic thread.
Attach a piece of card stock to the inside with a cut out window. *

Green Star Card

Cut the two sides of the outer star pattern from stencil EF8020. * (Incire)
Score the base of each triangle and using the Incire folding tool, fold back towards the center of the star.
Pierce a hole into each folded tip and the underlying card stock. Use the pattern provided at the beginning of the chapter, to embroider the star string art design.
Attach beads to each of these points as well. *
Pierce holes for beads on the tip of each that remains in the middle of the cut out design and above each point of the cut out design.
Attach the beads in all of these pierced holes. The middle row of beads will need to be individually attached so the thread does not show through the cut out pattern.
Pierce the corner designs using EF8012 stencil and embroider in gold metallic thread.
Place straight gold line stickers (841) between the embroidered corners to create a frame.
Place straight gold line stickers on each triangular cut and folded design
Place two overlapping gold stars (853) in the center of the design if desired.
Attach a piece of ivory card stock to the inside to cover the threads and show through the cutouts.

Miniature Cards

These 10 miniature cards were made with materials and supplies used throughout the book using all of the techniques. They are fun and quick to make and will add that special touch to your gifts and thank you notes.

All of the pastel cards are from Miniature series #1
All of the white cards are from Miniature series #2

Please refer to the following sets of General Instructions
- Parchment Paper Craft
- Spirelli String Art
- Iris Folding
- Embroidery on Paper
- Papuela Paper Weaving
- Sewing on Beads
- Incire Paper Cutting
- Ornare Paper Piercing

DESCRIPTION ON PAGE 88 ➤

Maple Leaf

Punch out the center of the maple leaf shape.

Cut 2.5 cm or 1" strips of paper from 4 papers found in package IVP2036 and fold in half lengthwise
Place the miniature card front side down on top of the folding pattern.
Complete the maple leaf. *
Use holographic ribbon or paper to finish the center of the design.
Cover the inside of the card with a small square of white card stock.

Materials Required
- Iris Folding Paper (IVP)
- Holographic paper/ribbon

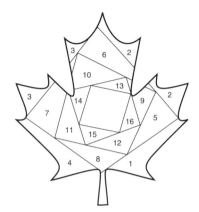

Flower

Punch out the petals of the flower however; leave the center circle in place.
Cut 3 cm or 1 1/4" strips of paper from IVP 2037 and fold in a half lengthwise.
Place miniature card front side down on top of pattern.
Place folded strips according to pattern and tape in place.
Complete the folding then pierce a hole from the front

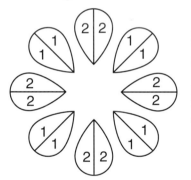

Materials Required
- Iris Folding Paper (IVP2037)
- Small white 3-D flower
- Blue Bead

through to the back and attach a small 3-D flower with a blue bead. *
Cover the inside of the card with a small square of white card stock.

Pink Baby Carriage

Punch out the center of the octagon frame.
Emboss the entire gift tag using the background template AE1201.
Center the baby carriage pattern for embroidery on the punched out octagon.
Pierce the baby carriage pattern. *
Emboss polka dots with AE1201 around the carriage if desired.
Embroider the pattern using pink thread as indicated. *
Place some double-sided tape on the back of the embroidered design. With the gift card closed place the embroidered design though the window in the card (this will align the center correctly) and attach to the back of the card. Add a ribbon as desired.

Materials Required
- Pattern from "A New Baby" Chapter
- Background stencil (AE1201)
- Pink Thread

Polka Dot Window

Punch out the 4 squares from the window card.

Emboss polka dots around the frame of the window.

Attach 1 medium blue, 1 medium green and one small blue layered 3-D flower to the center of the card using a yellow bead. *

Cut a piece of Pergamano parchment vellum slightly smaller than the card itself.

Emboss polka dots on the vellum to show through the 4 windowpanes.

Attach the vellum to the card stock using Perga glue or double-sided tape.

You may wish to emboss the envelope with polka dots as well before you fold it together. The example has the front and the closing flap embossed with polka dots.

Materials Required
- Pergamano Vellum
- Background Template (AE1201)
- Large embossing tool

Blue Baby Booties

Punch out the center of the circle frame.

Emboss the entire gift tag using the background template AE1201.

Center the baby booties on template PR0511 on the punched circle and pierce. *

Place some double-sided tape on the back of the pierced design. With the gift card closed place the pierced design though the window in the card (this will align the circle correctly) and attach to the back of the card. Add a ribbon as desired.

Materials Required
- Ornare baby template (PR0511)
- Ornare piercing tool

Pastel green parchment card

Punch out the square center of the card.

Using the pattern provided emboss the center flower design and corner leaf designs using Luper #7 onto parchment vellum. *

Emboss some shading with the small ball embossing tool in the bottom of the leaves and small lines from the center of the flower petals.

In the bottom of each of the leaf designs perforate (from the back) using the flower tool.

In the center of each side of the square use the star embossing tool and add a green dot to the center of the star embossing tool design with green ink or gel pen.

Perforate around each of the petals using the 2-needle tool or 2-needle split tool, leaving the bottom of the petal attached to the center of the flower. Cut out the perforations using your Pergamano scissors or very gently press out. Lift up each of the petals to make the flower 3-dimensional.

Materials Required
- Pergamano Luper #7 (1187)
- Parchment vellum
- Background Template (AE1201)
- Embossing Tools (medium, small ball)
- Star embossing tool
- Flower tool

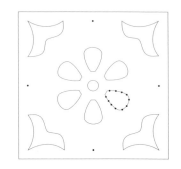

Pierce a hole through the center of the flower and sew on a bead.
Attach the embossed and perforated design to the back of the card so that the flower design shows through the window.
Attach a 2nd piece of vellum to the back to serve as a background for the perforated petals and cover the thread used to attach the bead.

Butterfly card

Punch out the center of the arched frame. Emboss the lower left corner and upper right corner with butterflies from EE3401. Center the butterfly pattern from EF8011 on the punched out arch.
Pierce and embroider the butterfly using yellow and green thread as indicated. *
Place some double-sided tape on the back of the embroidered design. With the gift card closed place the embroidered design though the window in the card (this will align it correctly) and attach to the back of the card. Add a ribbon as desired.

Materials Required
- Embossing Template EE3401
- Erica's Multipurpose stencil EF8011
- Medium embossing tool

Arched Window

Punch out the small squares from the window and the two arches.
On another piece of white card stock trace these openings and where to cut and fold the window to make an insert cover that will allow the window to open.
Cut out small pieces of printed vellum that

Materials Required
- Pergamano Vellum (1637)
- White card stock
- Erica's multipurpose stencil EF8009
- Blue Gel Pen

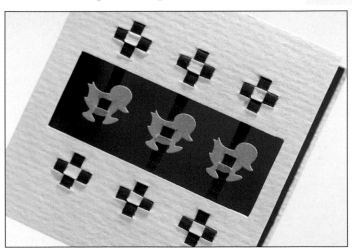

DESCRIPTION ON PAGE 96

DESCRIPTION ON PAGE 90 ▶

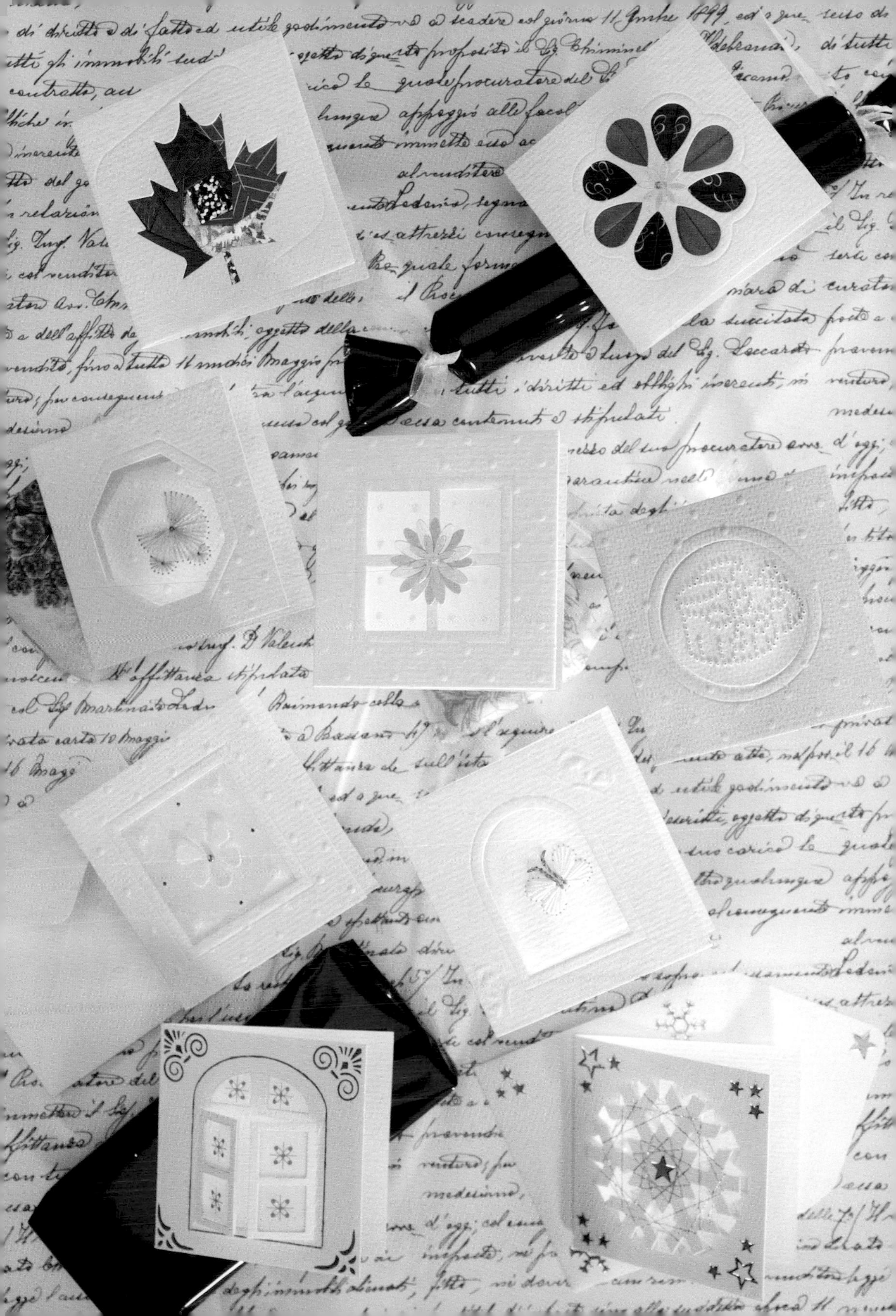

would make a nice design in the window. The example used Pergamano vellum (1637).

Carefully glue these small pieces of vellum into the open areas of the window. Attach the insert to the back to cover the edges and finish the card.

Decorate the corners of the card using Erica's multipurpose stencil EF8009 by coloring in the corner designs with a blue gel pen (see Chapter 4: Blue and White cards)

Snowflake

Punch out the snowflake from the miniature card.

Complete Spirelli string art using gold metallic thread according to the pattern. Complete the inner layer first, that is start at 3, follow the line come back up to 4 then follow the line down and continue in this fashion until the inner layer is complete. Then complete the outer layer according to the pattern.

Attach to the miniature card using 3mm foam blocks. The snowflake is offset from its original position by $1/4$ turn. Determine the correct position before attaching. Place the foam blocks a on the string art design then attach to ensure they will not show.

Decorate the corners and center of the snowflake with star stickers (853).

Decorate the envelope with stickers as desired.

Materials Required
- Gold Thread
- Stickers
- Foam blocks (3mm) (AV8938)

Papuela Duck Card

Center the Papuela template PU0021 on the card so that 3 weaving designs will fit.

Cut the weaving pattern into the card and cut out the window with a sharp hobby knife. *

Begin weaving the blue paper strips according to the pattern. For each center row of the designs take the paper strip across the window to the other side. First add a yellow duck tackie in the window then continue the weaving pattern on the opposite side. *

Complete all three designs as above.

Materials Required
- Papuela Template (PU0021)
- Blue Papuela strips (PU1101)
- Yellow Duck Tackies (PU1006)
- Red Paper (IC0402)

Attach a piece of red paper (the example used red and blue Incire duo punch paper, however you could use any red paper) to the entire inside of the card. The left side of the card needs to have the window cut into it and then will cover the weaving strips. The right side shows through the window setting off the card.